BASIC OCCUPATIONAL MATH

SECOND EDITION

W9-CCJ-879

David Newton

DEDICATION

Dedicated with love and appreciation to the memory
of Miss Lenore Bader and Miss Marion Campbell,
both master teachers within and beyond the classroom walls

1   2   3   4   5   6   7   8   9   10

ISBN 0-8251-4354-3

Copyright © 1990, 2002
J. Weston Walch, Publisher
P. O. Box 658 • Portland, Maine 04104-0658
www.walch.com

Printed in the United States of America

CONTENTS

To the Student

Mathematics is essential in almost every occupation. A plumber measures how much pipe to use on a job. A caterer decides how much food to order for a party. A farmer calculates how much seed, fertilizer, and pesticide to order. Math is part of the job, whether the job involves clerical work, construction, auto mechanics, medicine, banking, decorating, masonry, roofing, truck driving, flower arranging, dressmaking, or countless other skills.

Basic Occupational Math introduces you to the most important basic concepts of occupational mathematics. Each section of the book deals with a single area of mathematics, such as adding whole numbers or using percents. After a brief explanation, solved examples show how to use the mathematical concept to solve problems. Every chapter offers practice problems. You'll learn how to use the math to solve real-life issues that come up on the job.

Calculators are powerful tools. They do the math operations you need in any occupation. Of course, before you can use a calculator, you must understand the math.

For example, a painter has to calculate the area of a surface to be painted to estimate how much paint to buy. *Basic Occupational Math* shows how to use your calculator to solve problems like that. Once you learn the math, your calculator will do the work of multiplying, dividing, adding, and subtracting.

David E. Newton
Ashland, OR

CHAPTER ONE

WHOLE NUMBERS

Place Value in Numbers

Learning the Concept

The mathematical system we use consists of only 10 different numerals: 1, 2, 3, 4, 5, 6, 7, 8, 9, and 0. These numerals are also called *digits*. With these 10 numerals, we can create an unlimited number of actual numbers. For example, we can combine the numerals 3, 7, and 9 to make the number 379. The reason we can make so many numbers out of only 10 numerals is that, in the number system we use, numbers have *place value*. **Place value** means that the value of a numeral depends on where it appears in a number. In the number 379, for example, the position farthest to the right is the ones, or units, position.

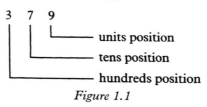

Figure 1.1

A numeral (such as the 9 in 379) in the units position simply has its own value: 9.

The next position to the left—the 7 in 379—is the tens position. Any number that appears in that position has its value multiplied by 10. Thus, the numeral 7 in 379 stands for 10×7, or 70 in this number.

The next position to the left—the 3 in 379—is the hundreds position. Any number in this position has its value multiplied by 100. Thus, the 3 in 379 stands for 100×3, or 300, in this number. The place value of numerals in very large numbers is shown in Figure 1.2:

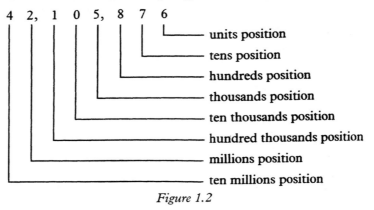

Figure 1.2

Thus, the number 42,105,876 can be thought of as:

	4 ten millions, or	40,000,000
+	2 millions, or	2,000,000
+	1 hundred thousand, or	100,000
+	0 ten thousands, or	00,000
+	5 thousands, or	5,000
+	8 hundreds, or	800
+	7 tens, or	70
+	6 units, or	6

Sometimes you have to use numbers smaller than 1. One way to write those numbers is with decimals. A **decimal** is a number less than 1, written with a decimal point. The number 0.5619 is a decimal. The dot following the 0 is a decimal point.

You can determine the place value of numerals in a decimal number just as you did with large whole numbers. In the case of decimal numbers, the first number to the right of the decimal point is in the tenths place. The meaning of the 5 in 0.5619, then, is 0.1×5, or 0.5.

Another way to think of the number 0.5619 is shown in Figure 1.3:

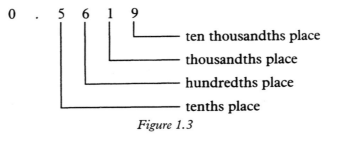

Figure 1.3

The meaning of the 6 in the hundredths place is 0.01×6, or 0.06. The value of the next two digits is determined as follows:

$$\text{thousandths: } 0.001 \times 1 = 0.001$$
$$\text{ten thousandths: } 0.000\,1 \times 9 = 0.000\,9$$

— Solved Examples —

EXAMPLE: Write the number 23,876, showing the actual value of every numeral in the number.

SOLUTION: 2 is in the ten thousands place, so $2 \times 10,000$ = 20,000
 3 is in the thousands place, so $3 \times 1,000$ = 3,000
 8 is in the hundreds place, so 8×100 =   800
 7 is in the tens place, so 7×10 =   70
 6 is in the units place, so 6×1 =   6
Therefore, $23,876 = 20,000 + 3,000 + 800 + 70 + 6$.

 *Practice Problems*

Write out the numbers below showing the value of every digit in the number.

a. 215

_____
_____
_____

b. 8,378

_____
_____
_____
_____

c. 63,479

_____
_____
_____
_____
_____

d. 813,721

_____
_____
_____
_____
_____
_____

e. 10,442,179

_____
_____
_____
_____
_____
_____
_____
_____

f. 50,070

_____
_____
_____
_____

g. 0.45

_____
_____

h. 0.037

_____
_____
_____

i. 2.38

_____
_____
_____

Adding Whole Numbers

Learning the Concept

Addition is the process of finding the *sum* of two or more numbers. Nearly every occupation requires that a person know how to add whole numbers. For example, a stock clerk might be asked to find the total number of books in a shipment. Suppose that one box in the shipment holds 50 books, a second box has 35 books, and a third box contains 47 books. The total number of books in the shipment can be found by adding these numbers:

Total number of books = 50 + 35 + 47 = 132 books

A carpenter might have to add two or more lengths to get the total length of a room. A secretary might have to use addition to find the total number of pages in six manuscripts. Or a lab technician might have to find the total volume of a solution made by combining three other solutions.

This section will show you how to add two or more numbers. Suppose you are asked to add the two numbers 132 and 346. The problem is set up as follows:

$$\begin{array}{r} 1\ 3\ 2 \\ +\ 3\ 4\ 6 \\ \hline \end{array}$$

The first step in this problem is to combine the digits in the units place: 2 + 6 = 8, or

$$\begin{array}{r} 1\ 3\ 2 \\ +\ 3\ 4\ 6 \\ \hline 8 \end{array}$$

Then combine the digits in the tens place: 3 + 4 = 7.

$$\begin{array}{r} 1\ 3\ 2 \\ +\ 3\ 4\ 6 \\ \hline 7\ 8 \end{array}$$

Then combine the digits in the hundreds place: 1 + 3 = 4.

$$\begin{array}{r} 1\ 3\ 2 \\ +\ 3\ 4\ 6 \\ \hline 4\ 7\ 8 \end{array}$$

The answer to the problem is 478.

A complication may arise. What happens in the addition problem below when you combine the digits in the units place?

$$\begin{array}{r} 2\ 4\ 5 \\ +\ 1\ 2\ 7 \\ \hline \end{array}$$

The combination of the digits in the units place is 5 + 7 = 12. But you can't put two digits in the units place (or in any other place). Only the 2 in the 12 belongs in the units place. The 1 belongs in the tens place. So, write

$$\begin{array}{r} 2\ ^{1}4\ 5 \\ +\ 1\ 2\ 7 \\ \hline 2 \end{array}$$

The small 1 above the 4 is "carried over" after adding the unit digits.

Now, when you add the tens digits, you have three numbers to include: 1 + 4 + 2, or

$$\begin{array}{r} 2\ ^{1}4\ 5 \\ +\ 1\ 2\ 7 \\ \hline 7\ 2 \end{array}$$

Conclude by adding the hundreds digits.

$$\begin{array}{r} 2\ ^{1}4\ 5 \\ +\ 1\ 2\ 7 \\ \hline 3\ 7\ 2 \end{array}$$

The answer to the problem 245 + 127 is 372. As you become more skilled in doing addition problems, you will no longer have to write down the carried number. You will remember it in your head.

— Solved Examples —

EXAMPLE A: Two boxes of books have arrived in the shipping room. One box contains 258 books. The other holds 365 books. What is the total number of books in the two boxes?

SOLUTION: To solve this problem, first arrange the numbers so that they can be added. Place the numbers one above the other so that the units place of one number is above the units place of the other, the tens place of one is above the tens place of the other, and so on.

$$\begin{array}{r} 2\ 5\ 8\ \text{books} \\ +\ 3\ 6\ 5\ \text{books} \\ \hline \end{array}$$

Now begin adding at the units place: 8 + 5 = 13. Put the 3 in the units place of the answer, and carry over the 1 in the tens place.

$$\begin{array}{r} 2\ ^{1}5\ 8\ \text{books} \\ +\ 3\ 6\ 5\ \text{books} \\ \hline 3 \end{array}$$

Addition in the tens place gives 1 + 5 + 6 = 12. Put the 2 in the tens place in the answer and carry over the 1 to the hundreds place.

$$^{1}2 \ ^{1}5 \ 8 \quad \text{books}$$
$$+ \ 3 \ 6 \ 5 \quad \text{books}$$
$$\overline{ 2 \ 3 \quad \text{books}}$$

Finally, add the digits in the hundreds place: 1 + 2 + 3 = 6.

$$^{1}2 \ ^{1}5 \ 8 \quad \text{books}$$
$$+ \ 3 \ 6 \ 5 \quad \text{books}$$
$$\overline{6 \ 2 \ 3 \quad \text{books}}$$

The total number of books is 258 + 365 = 623.

EXAMPLE B: Use a calculator to add 479 and 88.

SOLUTION (USING A CALCULATOR): To add 479 and 88, complete the following steps:

1. Clear display. | C |

2. Enter the first number. | 4 | | 7 | | 9 |

3. Press the addition key. | + |

4. Enter the second number. | 8 | | 8 |

5. Press the equals key. | = |

6. Read the answer on the display.   5 6 7

NOTE: Calculators do not all operate the same way. Ask your instructor for help if the method described above does not work with your calculator.

Practice Problems

1. Add the following numbers:

a.	4 2	b.	6 8 1	c.	7 5	d.	3 6 9
	+ 1 3		+ 3 0 5		+ 2 7		+ 4 9 8

e. 32 + 47 _____

f. 691 + 843 _____

g. 624 + 585 + 710 _____

h. 81 + 310 + 4,071 _____

i. 169 + 4,785 + 328 _____

j. 16,248 + 2,898 + 13,342 _____

k. 284 + 5,871 + 395 + 26 _____

2. Francesco needs 328 bricks to build one part of a wall, 469 bricks to build a second part of the wall, and 98 bricks to build the third part of the wall. What is the total number of bricks needed to build the wall?

_____

3. Darlene is purchasing pipe for work at the six locations listed below. What is the total amount of pipe she will need for these jobs?
    Hennessey house: 158 feet   Waldron house: 216 feet
    Mayhew Company: 2,572 feet   Wellspring Company: 3,428 feet
    Gibbens house: 329 feet   Durant house: 652 feet

_____

4. Luis is ordering flour for the bakery to use this month. The bakers say they will need 94 pounds of flour the first week, 129 pounds the second week, 88 pounds the third week, and 147 pounds the fourth week. To be on the safe side, Luis wants to order 25 extra pounds of flour. What is the total weight of flour he should order for the month?

_____

5. In Figure 1.4, the dimensions *a, b,* and *c* are all 13 mm in length, *d* and *g* are 25 mm, and *e* and *f* are 27 mm each. What is the total length, *l,* of the figure?

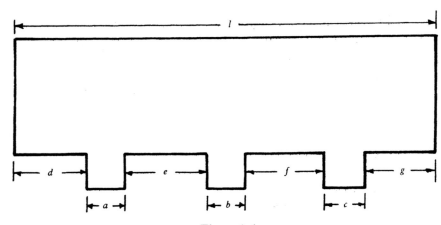

Figure 1.4

6. Frannie's job is to compile orders from seven branch stores of the Sunset Garden Supply Company. How many iris bulbs should she order if the seven branches have sent in requests for 160 bulbs, 192 bulbs, 236 bulbs, 95 bulbs, 148 bulbs, 185 bulbs, and 248 bulbs?

7. One of Li's jobs in the Roxie Theater's business office is to tabulate the number of tickets sold per hour and daily at the box office. On Tuesday, 158 tickets were sold at 5 P.M.; 1,498 tickets at 6 P.M.; 293 tickets at 7 P.M.; 1,987 tickets at 8 P.M.; 349 tickets at 9 P.M.; and 1,939 tickets at 10 P.M. What was the total number of tickets sold on Tuesday?

8. What is the total length of fencing needed to enclose the lot shown in Figure 1.5?

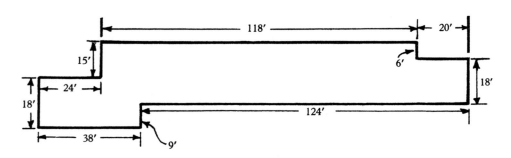

Figure 1.5

9. Windows of six standard sizes are being installed at the Horvath Building. From the specification sheet below, what is the total number of windows of each kind needed for all six floors?

_____

Floor	Size A	Size B	Size C	Size D	Size E	Size F
1	8	8	8	8	8	8
2	24	32	48	48	32	24
3	16	16	32	32	48	48
4	8	8	16	8	8	16
5	5	15	15	15	15	15
6	9	18	9	18	9	18

10. The new fiber optic cable being laid in Danbury County will be put down in eight sections. The length of each section is as follows: 1: 350 m; 2: 475 m; 3: 95 m; 4: 350 m; 5: 585 m; 6: 685 m; 7: 79 m; 8: 597 m. What is the total length of the cable to be laid?

_____

Subtracting Whole Numbers

Learning the Concept

Subtraction is the process by which one quantity is taken away from another. After subtraction, a quantity is "left over" or "remaining." Knowing how to subtract is necessary in nearly every occupation. For example, an electrician may cut a piece of wire 34 feet long from a spool that contains 180 feet of wire. To find out how much wire remains on the spool, the electrician must subtract 34 feet from 180 feet.

A baker can find out how much flour is left in a bin after she removes some flour for baking by subtraction. A farmer can calculate the amount of his field that still needs to be planted by subtracting the amount that has already been planted. A stock clerk can find out how many books are left in a stockroom by subtracting the amount she has removed from the total in the room to begin with.

The example below shows you how to do a subtraction problem.

$$\begin{array}{r} 5\ 8\ 3 \\ -\ 4\ 1\ 2 \\ \hline \end{array}$$

In this problem, the top number is known as the **minuend,** the lower number is the **subtrahend,** and the answer is known as the **difference.** You can solve this problem by subtracting one place at a time, starting from the right. In the units place, 2 subtracted from 3 is 1.

$$\begin{array}{r} 5\ 8\ 3 \\ -\ 4\ 1\ 2 \\ \hline 1 \end{array}$$

In the tens place, 1 subtracted from 8 is 7.

$$\begin{array}{r} 5\ 8\ 3 \\ -\ 4\ 1\ 2 \\ \hline 7\ 1 \end{array}$$

And in the hundreds place, 4 subtracted from 5 is 1.

$$\begin{array}{r} 5\ 8\ 3 \\ -\ 4\ 1\ 2 \\ \hline 1\ 7\ 1 \end{array}$$

The answer is 171.

Sometimes you do not have enough in the minuend to allow subtraction directly. For example, consider this problem:

$$
\begin{array}{r}
3\ 7\ 4 \\
-\ 1\ 2\ 9 \\
\hline
\end{array}
$$

You cannot subtract 9 from 4. But you can go next door to the tens place and borrow one of the tens from that place. Think of the problem in this way:

$$
\begin{array}{r}
3\ 7\ 4 \\
-\ 1\ 2\ 9 \\
\hline
\end{array}
\longrightarrow
\begin{array}{r}
3\ 6^{+1}4 \\
-\ 1\ 2\ 9 \\
\hline
\end{array}
\longrightarrow
\begin{array}{r}
3\ 6\ {}^{1}4 \\
-\ 1\ 2\ 9 \\
\hline
\end{array}
$$

Removing one numeral from the tens place ($1 \times 10 = 10$) and transferring it to the units place gives you 14, the 4 from the original number (374) plus the 10 that has been borrowed. Now you can subtract 9 from 14.

$$
\begin{array}{r}
3\ 6\ {}^{1}4 \\
-\ 1\ 2\ 9 \\
\hline
5
\end{array}
$$

Continue as before, subtracting 2 from 6, then 1 from 3, to get the answer.

$$
\begin{array}{r}
3\ 6\ {}^{1}4 \\
-\ 1\ 2\ 9 \\
\hline
2\ 4\ 5
\end{array}
$$

The answer to the problem is 245. As you become experienced, you will no longer have to scratch out one number and write in the transferred 1. You will do the borrowing in your head.

— Solved Examples —

EXAMPLE A: Of 289 televisions sold the week before Christmas, 97 were returned the week after Christmas. How many TVs were *not* returned?

SOLUTION: The number of TVs not returned is

$$
\begin{array}{r}
2\ 8\ 9 \\
-\ 9\ 7 \\
\hline
\end{array}
$$

Subtract by starting at the right, with the units place.

$$
\begin{array}{r}
2\ 8\ 9 \\
-\ 9\ 7 \\
\hline
2
\end{array}
$$

Then move left, to the tens place. It is not possible to subtract 9 from 8. So borrow a 1 from the hundreds place and transfer it to the tens place. When you do so, you have a 1 left in the hundreds place and an additional 10 in the tens place.

$$\begin{array}{r} {}^1\!2\ {}^1\!8\ 9 \\ -\ \ 9\ 7 \\ \hline 2 \end{array}$$

Now you can subtract 9 from 18 and get the answer:

$$\begin{array}{r} {}^1\!2\ {}^1\!8\ 9 \\ -\ \ 9\ 7 \\ \hline 1\ 9\ 2 \end{array}$$

The answer is 192 TVs were not returned.

EXAMPLE B: Subtract 348 from 579 using a calculator.

SOLUTION (USING A CALCULATOR): To subtract 348 from 579, complete the following steps:

1. Clear display. | C |

2. Enter the minuend. | 5 | | 7 | | 9 |

3. Press the subtraction key. | − |

4. Enter the subtrahend. | 3 | | 4 | | 8 |

5. Press the equals key. | = |

6. Read the answer on the display.   231

Practice Problems

1. Subtract the following numbers.

a.	6 9	b.	8 7 4	c.	5 3	d.	2, 3 1 8	e.	3, 0 4 5
	− 5 4		− 3 2 1		− 3 7		− 1, 1 8 3		− 2, 8 8 7

f. 858 − 421 _____

g. 763 − 587 _____

h. 1,047 − 768 _____

i. 36,151 − 8,923 _____

j. 115,467 − 7,884 _____

2. How much does the head add to the total length of the bolt shown in Figure 1.6?

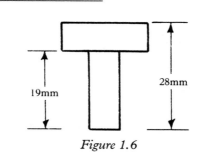

Figure 1.6

3. In Thursday's manufacture of 17,482 transistors, 629 were found to be defective. How many were not defective?

4. A truck delivering waste newspapers to a recycling plant weighs in at 32,482 pounds when full and 19,894 pounds when empty. What is the weight of the newspapers in the truck?

5. Hua works as an assistant to a landscape architect. He has been told to spread 250 pounds of grass seed on a new lawn, but finds that he has only 192 pounds of seed in storage. How much additional seed must he order?

6. What is the length of the section marked x on the aluminum extrusion shown in Figure 1.7?

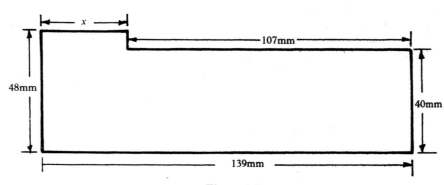

Figure 1.7

7. What is the width of the fiber gasket (shaded area) shown in the diagram in Figure 1.8?

_____

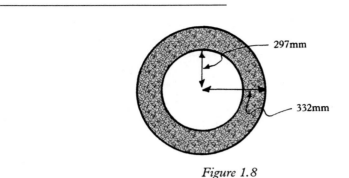

Figure 1.8

8. For a wiring job in a new house, Nick cuts four sections of wire from a spool 300 feet long. The sections are 42 feet, 79 feet, 32 feet, and 66 feet in length. How much wire remains on the spool?

_____

9. Susan has given out turpentine to four workers on her paint crew in the following amounts: Anna, 11 liters; Bob, 17 liters; Frank, 14 liters; and Judy, 19 liters. How much turpentine is left from the original 75 liters?

_____

10. Andy has driven his truck from Watts to Red River on the route shown in Figure 1.9. How much farther does he still have to drive to reach Dawson? The distance from Watts to Dawson is 176 miles.

_____

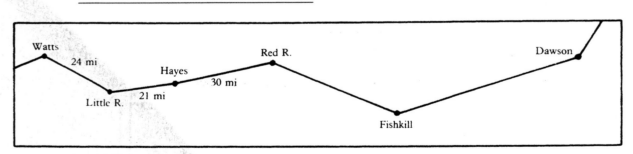

Figure 1.9

Multiplying Whole Numbers

Learning the Concept

Workers in many occupations use multiplication every day. A mason calculates the number of bricks in a shipment by multiplying the number of boxes in the shipment times the number of bricks in each box. A nurse finds the total amount of medication given to a patient by multiplying the amount of medicine in one dose times the number of doses. A truck driver determines his weekly pay by multiplying his hourly pay times the number of hours worked during the week.

Multiplication is a form of addition. The multiplication problem 21×5 really means to add 21 five times, or:

$$21 + 21 + 21 + 21 + 21$$

To do multiplication problems, you must memorize the basic multiplication tables. Most people learn the tables through the 12s. When you have memorized all the one-number-by-one-number multiplications, you can go on to more difficult multiplication problems.

A Typical Multiplication Table

	1	2	3	4	5	6	7	8	9
1	1	2	3	4	5	6	7	8	9
2	2	4	6	8	10	12	14	16	18
3	3	6	9	12	15	18	21	24	27
4	4	8	12	16	20	24	28	32	36
5	5	10	15	20	25	30	35	40	45
6	6	12	18	24	30	36	42	48	54
7	7	14	21	28	35	42	49	56	63
8	8	16	24	32	40	48	56	64	72
9	9	18	27	36	45	54	63	72	81

The easiest place to begin is with multiplying a two-digit number by a one-digit number. For example:

$$
\begin{array}{r}
2\ 1 \\
\times\ 3 \\
\hline
\end{array}
$$

To solve this problem, start multiplying from the right and move to the left. Begin with $1 \times 3 = 3$.

$$
\begin{array}{r}
2\ 1 \\
\times\ 3 \\
\hline
3
\end{array}
$$

Then, move to the left and multiply $2 \times 3 = 6$.

$$
\begin{array}{r}
2\ 1 \\
\times\ 3 \\
\hline
6\ 3
\end{array}
$$

The answer is $21 \times 3 = 63$.

A more difficult problem is to multiply 36 by 2. Follow the same steps as before. Starting at the right, multiply 6×2, which equals 12. But only the 2 in this answer can go in the units place. The 1 belongs in the tens place. So it has to be carried over to the tens position.

$$
\begin{array}{r}
{}^{1}3\ 6 \\
\times\ 2 \\
\hline
2
\end{array}
$$

Now move to the left and multiply 3×2, which gives you 6 in the tens place. But remember that you have already carried over 1 from the first multiplication. So the total in the tens place is $6 + 1$, or 7.

$$
\begin{array}{r}
3\ 6 \\
\times\ 2 \\
\hline
7\ 2
\end{array}
$$

The answer to the problem 36×2 is 72.

Use the same steps to multiply by a two-digit number. For example, suppose you have to multiply 54 by 23. Here are the steps to follow.

To begin, ignore the 2 and multiply the top number, 54, by 3.

$$
\begin{array}{r}
\mathbf{5\ 4} \\
\times\ \mathbf{2\ 3} \\
\hline
\end{array}
$$

Start at the right and multiply 4×3 to get 12. Write down the 2 and carry the 1 to the tens place.

$$
\begin{array}{r}
{}^{1}5\ 4 \\
\times\ 2\ 3 \\
\hline
2
\end{array}
$$

Then, multiply 5×3 to get 15. Don't forget to add the 1 carried over from the first multiplication.

$$
\begin{array}{r}
5\ 4 \\
\times\ 2\ 3 \\
\hline
1\ 6\ 2
\end{array}
$$

Now, multiply the top number, 54, by the 2 in 23. Starting at the right, $4 \times 2 = 8$. Notice that the 2 you multiply is in the tens place, so the answer also has to be in the tens place.

$$
\begin{array}{r}
5\ 4 \\
\times\ 2\ 3 \\
\hline
1\ 6\ 2 \\
8
\end{array}
$$

Then multiply 5×2 to get 10.

$$
\begin{array}{r}
5\ 4 \\
\times\ 2\ 3 \\
\hline
1\ 6\ 2 \\
1\ 0\ 8
\end{array}
$$

Notice how important it is to line up the numbers you have found so far. The tens digits (in this example, 6 and 8) must be lined up, and the hundreds digits (1 and 0) also have to be lined up.

To complete the problem, simply add the results of the two multiplications.

$$
\begin{array}{r}
5\ 4 \\
\times\ 2\ 3 \\
\hline
1\ 6\ 2 \\
1\ 0\ 8 \\
\hline
1\ 2\ 4\ 2
\end{array}
$$

The answer to the problem 54×23 is 1,242.

A Note about Multiplication Symbols

In the problems above, we have used the symbol × to represent multiplication. But other symbols can also be used to represent multiplication. Another symbol used to indicate multiplication is a dot centered between two numbers (·). For example, the problem 13×45 can also be written as $13 \cdot 45$.

Parentheses can also be used to represent multiplication. For example, 13×45 can also be written as $(13)(45)$ or $(13) \cdot (45)$.

Finally, two or more letters written next to each other can also stand for multiplication. The formula for the area of a rectangle, area = length × width, for example, is $A = lw$. In this formula, lw means $l \times w$.

Now you can see that the formula for the area of a rectangle can be written in four different ways, all of which mean exactly the same thing:

Area = length × width, or $A = l \times w$

or $A = l \cdot w$

or $A = (l)(w)$

or $A = (l) \cdot (w)$

or $A = lw$

— Solved Examples —

EXAMPLE A: Every worker in Louisa's knitting factory will use 32 skeins of yarn in one day. How many skeins will each worker use altogether during a month of 24 workdays?

SOLUTION: The total number of skeins can be found by multiplying 32 skeins by 24 workdays.

$$
\begin{array}{r}
3\ 2 \text{ skeins} \\
\times\ 2\ 4 \text{ workdays} \\
\hline
\end{array}
$$

Multiplying the top number by 4 gives

$$
\begin{array}{r}
3\ 2 \text{ skeins} \\
\times\ 2\ 4 \text{ workdays} \\
\hline
1\ 2\ 8
\end{array}
$$

Multiplying the top number by 2, and keeping the answer in its proper position, gives

$$
\begin{array}{r}
3\ 2 \text{ skeins} \\
\times\ 2\ 4 \text{ workdays} \\
\hline
1\ 2\ 8 \\
6\ 4
\end{array}
$$

Adding the two partial answers gives

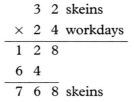

$$\begin{array}{r} 3\ 2 \text{ skeins} \\ \times\ 2\ 4 \text{ workdays} \\ \hline 1\ 2\ 8 \\ 6\ 4 \\ \hline 7\ 6\ 8 \text{ skeins} \end{array}$$

Thus, 768 skeins of yarn are used in one month.

EXAMPLE B: Multiply 532 by 87 using a calculator.

SOLUTION:

1. Clear display.

2. Enter the number to be multiplied.

3. Press the multiplication key.

4. Enter the multiplier.

5. Press the equals key.

6. Read the answer on the display.

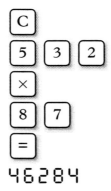

Practice Problems

1. Perform the following multiplications.

   a.   2 3
        × 2
        —————

   b.   1 3 2
          × 8
        —————

   c.   6 8
        × 3 5
        —————

   d.   2 3 3
        × 3 4
        —————

   e.   7 9 8
        × 8 5
        —————

   f.   3 7 9
        × 2 2 5
        —————

   g. 32 × 64 × 19 _____

   h. 482 × 36 × 216 _____

2. Arnie has 8 men and women working for him in his printing plant. Each worker put in 45 hours of work last week. What was the total number of hours worked by all workers together during the week?

   _____

3. Geraldine has learned that she uses 275 nails on her carpentry job on an average day. How many nails should she order for a job that will take her 18 days to complete?

   _____

4. Each mechanic in Arturo's auto shop uses an average of 132 spark plugs per week. How many spark plugs must he order altogether for his 18 mechanics each week? How many does he order in one 52-week year?

   _____

5. During Melanie's busiest week at the florist shop, she uses 8 carnations, 9 roses, and 13 sprigs of greenery in every Melanie's Special bouquet she makes. If she plans to sell 275 of these special bouquets during that week, how many of each of the three items should she order?

   _____

6. The packages of tiles Kwon needs on a job consist of 6 tiles per section, 48 sections per box. How many tiles are there in his current supply of 97 boxes of tiles?

   _____

7. Chris's printing shop uses an average of 85 reams of paper per week. How many sheets of paper does the shop use in a typical 48-week year? (*Hint:* Look up the number of sheets in one ream of paper.)

_____

8. The transistors used in Vicki's shop are shipped 28 to the box. The chart below shows the number of boxes used by each of her repair teams last month. Calculate the total number of transistors used by each team in the shop last month.

Week	*Team 1*	*Team 2*	*Team 3*	*Team 4*
1	8	7	13	11
2	9	21	12	13
3	5	9	17	16
4	14	13	13	11

_____

9. Frank is foreman of a production section that produces rolls of aluminum sheeting that weigh 324 pounds each. The table below shows the production record of three teams in Frank's section for last week. Calculate the total weight of aluminum produced by each team in Frank's section last week.

Rolls of aluminum produced

Team	Monday	Tuesday	Wednesday	Thursday	Friday
1	56	55	38	48	47
2	32	49	39	39	37
3	45	51	37	50	47

_____

10. The peas harvested by Aurelio's crew weigh 27 pounds per bushel. How many pounds of peas did each person in Aurelio's crew harvest last month?

Bushels of peas harvested

Team Member	Week 1	Week 2	Week 3	Week 4
Elaine	112	135	116	129
Sam	107	114	119	105
Carlos	137	126	119	103

_____

Dividing Whole Numbers

Learning the Concept

Division lets you find the number of times one quantity must be multiplied to obtain another quantity. Division is the opposite of multiplication.

Division problems are common in many occupations. A painter might want to divide 200 gallons of paint among 8 workers. She can find out how much paint each worker gets by dividing 200 gallons by 8 workers. A truck driver can find his average speed by dividing the distance he travels by his time on the road. A caterer calculates the number of shrimp each person at a party gets by dividing the total number of shrimp by the number of people at the party. The following example shows how to carry out a division problem.

Suppose you are asked to divide 391 by 17. One way to write that problem is: 391 ÷ 17, where ÷ is called a division sign. The first step is to set up the problem as shown below. The number to be divided, 391 in this problem, goes inside the division sign. That number is called the **dividend.** The number by which the dividend is divided, 17 in this problem, goes outside the division sign. That number is called the **divisor.**

The first step in this division is to ask how many times the divisor will go into the first two numbers of the dividend. Ask: How many times does 17 go into 39? The answer is twice. Write the 2 above the 9 in 391.

$$
\begin{array}{r}
2 \\
17\overline{\smash{\big)}\,3\ 9\ 1}
\end{array}
$$

Now multiply the partial answer (2) times the divisor (17) and write the answer under the dividend.

$$
\begin{array}{r}
2 \\
17\overline{\smash{\big)}\,3\ 9\ 1} \\
3\ 4
\end{array}
$$

Subtract the partial product (34) from the first part of the dividend, as shown, and bring down the next number in the dividend (1).

$$
\begin{array}{r}
2 \\
17\overline{\smash{\big)}\,3\ 9\ 1} \\
\underline{3\ 4} \\
5\ 1
\end{array}
$$

Repeat the process just described. Ask how many times the divisor (17) goes into the partial dividend (51). The answer is 3, which you write above the next number (1) in the dividend.

```
        2 3
17 | 3 9 1
      3 4
      ‾‾‾
        5 1
```

Multiply the 3 times the divisor (17) and write down the next partial product (51). Subtract this partial product (51) from the partial dividend (51) and get 0.

```
        2 3
17 | 3 9 1
      3 4
      ‾‾‾
        5 1
        5 1
        ‾‾‾
          0
```

The answer: 391 divided by 17 is 23.

— Solved Examples —

EXAMPLE A: Gus's shoe factory produced 1,058 pairs of shoes during the month of July. How many pairs did it produce, on average, each of the 23 working days of the month?

SOLUTION: Divide the total number of pairs of shoes produced (1,058) by the number of working days (23).

```
          4 6
23 | 1 0 5 8
        9 2
        ‾‾‾
        1 3 8
        1 3 8
        ‾‾‾‾‾
            0
```

The answer is that the shoe factory produced an average of 46 pairs of shoes each working day.

EXAMPLE B: Doctor Kwan has asked Fred to divide a container of glucose solution holding 2,500 mL among 15 jars of equal size. What size jars should Fred use to hold these 15 portions?

SOLUTION: The problem is to find the volume that will be produced by dividing 2,500 mL into 15 equal-size jars. That is, divide 2,500 mL by 15.

```
15 | 2 5 0 0  mL
```

Your work will show you that 2,500 mL cannot be divided by 15 an exact number of times. Instead, 2,500 mL divided by 15 gives an answer of 166 with something left over.

$$
\begin{array}{r}
1\ 6\ 6\phantom{\ \text{mL}} \\
15\overline{)2\ 5\ 0\ 0}\ \text{mL} \\
\underline{1\ 5} \\
1\ 0\ 0 \\
\underline{9\ 0} \\
1\ 0\ 0 \\
\underline{9\ 0} \\
1\ 0
\end{array}
$$

The extra 10 in this problem is usually written as a fractional part of the divisor; for example, $\frac{10}{15}$. The answer to the division problem, then, is $166\frac{10}{15}$. You may already know that this fraction can be written in a simpler form. That is, $\frac{10}{15}$ is the same as $\frac{2}{3}$. So you can also write the answer as $166\frac{2}{3}$. So each jar must hold more than $166\frac{2}{3}$ mL.

EXAMPLE C: Divide 2,015 by 52 using a calculator.

SOLUTION:

1. Clear display.

2. Enter the dividend.

3. Press the division key.

4. Enter the divisor.

5. Press the equals key.

6. Read the answer on the display.

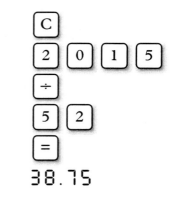

Practice
Problems

1. Perform the indicated divisions.

   a. 8 | 1 8 4

   b. 189 ÷ 7 _____

   c. 2 1 | 7 3 5

   d. 4,140 ÷ 45 _____

   e. 3,604 ÷ 53 _____

   f. 2,147 ÷ 19 _____

   g. 8,613 ÷ 87 _____

   h. 813 ÷ 35 _____

   i. 8,513 ÷ 989 _____

   j. 2,009 ÷ 32 _____

2. Evangeline has earned $490 while working 35 hours on a special nursing assignment. What was her hourly rate of pay?

3. Muriel has received a large shipment of 578 pairs of shoes in 17 cartons. If each carton holds the same amount, how many pairs of shoes are there in each carton?

4. The electric shop Arturo owns used 1,147 kwh of electricity during the month of January. How much did the shop use, on average, each day of the month?

5. In rearranging his office files, Milo finds that he has 1,134 files to store in 9 filing cabinets. Each filing cabinet has 3 drawers. If they are to be spread out equally among all drawers, how many files should go into each drawer?

6. Dan's truck weighs in at 51,480 pounds on a state scale. The empty truck weighs 19,875 pounds and carries 215 boxes of live turkeys. How much does each box of turkeys weigh? If there are 8 turkeys in each box, what is the average weight of one turkey?

7. Debbie's service station pumped 31,485 gallons of gas in August, 32,974 gallons in September, and 29,487 gallons in October. How much gas was pumped on an average day in each of those months?

8. Hwang's new restaurant has been open for six months. During that time, he has served a total of 6,840 appetizers, 8,460 entrees, 3,420 desserts, and 10,620 beverages. What was the average number of each food item sold each day? (Assume 30 days in a month.)

9. How many aluminum blanks of the design shown in Figure 1.10 can be produced from a piece of metal 100 m long? (1 m = 1,000 mm.)

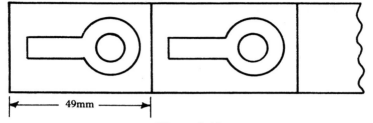

49mm

Figure 1.10

10. The table below shows the number of precision instruments produced by each of three teams at Alco Electronics last week. Over the course of the week, how many units, on average, were produced by each member of Vanna's team? By each member of Pat's team? By each member of Richard's team?

Production Count

Team Captain	Number of Team Members	Monday	Wednesday	Friday
Vanna	31	422	487	453
Pat	29	431	437	447
Richard	28	397	407	416

Vanna's team _____

Pat's team _____

Richard's team _____

CHAPTER TWO

FRACTIONS

Fraction Terminology

Learning the Concept

The first step in working with fractions is understanding the words to use. This section explains those terms for you.

1. A **fraction** is a part of a whole.

2. A fraction consists of two parts, called **terms,** one written above the other, as in the fraction

$$\frac{2}{9}$$

   The number above the line is the **numerator.** The number below the line is the **denominator.** A fraction written in this way is sometimes called a **common fraction.**

3. Common fractions can be written another way. For example, the common fraction shown above can be written as 2/9. The slanted line, /, in the fraction means the same thing as the horizontal line, —, in the fraction above. In both cases, the horizontal line, —, and the slanting line, /, mean *divided by.* So 2/9 really means 2 *divided by* 9.

   Here's another way of understanding what the fraction $\frac{2}{9}$ means. Suppose we cut an object, such as a pie, into nine equal parts. Then we remove two pieces of the pie. The parts that are missing make up two parts of the nine, or $\frac{2}{9}$ of the whole.

4. In a **proper fraction,** the numerator is smaller than or equal to the denominator. The fraction $\frac{2}{9}$ is a proper fraction because 2 is smaller than 9. The fraction $\frac{13}{32}$ is also a proper fraction. In an **improper fraction,** the numerator is larger than the denominator. The fraction $\frac{8}{7}$ is an improper fraction; so is $\frac{21}{10}$.

5. A **mixed number** consists of a whole number and a fraction. The number $1\frac{3}{4}$ is a mixed number; so is $28\frac{4}{15}$.

An improper fraction can always be changed to a mixed number, and vice versa. To change an improper fraction to a mixed number, remember the meaning of the horizontal line, —, or slanting line, /, in the fraction. Those lines mean *divided by*. For example:

$$\frac{8}{7} \text{ means } 8 \div 7, \text{ or } \quad 7\overline{\smash{)}8} = 1\frac{1}{7}$$

To change a mixed number to an improper fraction, multiply the denominator times the whole number. Then add the numerator. Write the answer over the denominator. For example, to change the mixed number $1\frac{3}{4}$ to an improper fraction:

First, multiply the denominator (4) times the whole number (1): $4 \times 1 = 4$.

Second, add the numerator (3): $4 + 3 = 7$.

Third, write the answer over the denominator (4): $\frac{7}{4}$.

Therefore, $1\frac{3}{4} = \frac{7}{4}$.

6. The fundamental rule of fractions is that you can multiply or divide *both* numerator and denominator by the same number without changing the value of the fraction. For example, begin with the fraction $\frac{1}{2}$. In example B below, both numerator and denominator have been multiplied by 3. The new fraction $\frac{3}{6}$ has the same value as $\frac{1}{2}$. In examples C and D, both numerator and denominator have been multiplied by 5 (C) and by 20 (D), respectively. All the fractions have exactly the same value.

$$\begin{array}{cccc} A & B & C & D \\ \frac{1}{2} & = \frac{3}{6} & = \frac{5}{10} & = \frac{20}{40} \end{array}$$

7. Fractions that have the same value, such as fractions A, B, C, and D, are **equivalent fractions.** Changing a fraction so that its numerator and denominator cannot be divided by any number is called *reducing a fraction to its lowest terms.* Fractions B, C, and D can all be reduced to lower terms, $\frac{1}{2}$. Fraction A is already in its lowest terms.

A Note about Fractions and Calculators

Many calculators do not display fractions. Calculators most often display only decimals. Chapter 3 discusses how to use calculators in working with decimals.

— Solved Examples —

EXAMPLE A: Change the improper fraction $\frac{31}{8}$ to a mixed number.

SOLUTION: Divide the numerator (31) by the denominator (8):

$$
\begin{array}{r}
3 \\
8\overline{\smash{\big)}\,3\ 1} \\
\underline{2\ 4} \\
7
\end{array}
$$

Answer: $\frac{31}{8} = 3\frac{7}{8}$.

EXAMPLE B: Change the mixed number $11\frac{2}{5}$ to an improper fraction.

SOLUTION: Multiply the denominator (5) times the whole number (11).

$$5 \times 11 \;=\; 55.$$

Then add the numerator.

$$55 + 2 = 57.$$

Finally, write the answer over the denominator (5).

$$\frac{57}{5}$$

Answer: $11\frac{2}{5}$ is equal to $\frac{57}{5}$.

EXAMPLE C: Reduce the fraction $\frac{48}{64}$ to its lowest terms.

SOLUTION: Divide both numerator and denominator by any number that goes into both evenly; for example, 2.

$$\frac{48 \div 2}{64 \div 2} \;=\; \frac{24}{32}$$

Can the numerator and denominator still both be divided evenly by some number? The answer is yes, 2.

$$\frac{24 \div 2}{32 \div 2} \;=\; \frac{12}{16}$$

You can probably see that the fraction $\frac{12}{16}$ can be reduced even further by dividing both numerator and denominator by 2, giving $\frac{6}{8}$. This fraction, $\frac{6}{8}$, can be reduced further by dividing both numerator and denominator by 2 again, giving $\frac{3}{4}$. But $\frac{3}{4}$ cannot be reduced any further. There is no number that goes evenly into both numerator (3) and denominator (4).

The process of reducing a fraction to its lowest terms goes more quickly if you can find the *largest* number that divides evenly into both numerator and denominator. If we had used 16 as the divisor for both numerator and denominator in the first step, we would have had an answer right away.

$$\frac{48 \div 16}{64 \div 16} \;=\; \frac{3}{4}$$

Practice Problems

1. In each of the following fractions:

   (1) Name the numerator (N).

   (2) Name the denominator (D).

   (3) Tell which fractions are proper fractions.

   (4) Tell which fractions are improper fractions.

   (5) Tell which are mixed numbers.

   (6) Tell which fractions are equivalent fractions.

   (7) Tell which fractions are in lowest terms.

   a. $\frac{2}{3}$ b. $1\frac{1}{6}$ c. $\frac{4}{6}$ d. $\frac{5}{2}$ e. $2\frac{2}{3}$ f. $\frac{32}{15}$

2. Change each of the following improper fractions to an equivalent mixed number.

   a. $\frac{3}{2}$ _____   b. $\frac{13}{5}$ _____   c. $\frac{23}{7}$ _____   d. $\frac{61}{5}$ _____   e. $\frac{132}{7}$ _____

3. Change each of the following mixed numbers to an equivalent improper fraction.

   a. $1\frac{1}{4}$ _____   b. $5\frac{1}{7}$ _____   c. $9\frac{3}{5}$ _____   d. $3\frac{7}{19}$ _____   e. $23\frac{2}{13}$ _____

4. Reduce each of the following fractions to lowest terms. If the fraction is already in lowest terms, write OK.

   a. $\frac{2}{8}$ _____   b. $\frac{8}{18}$ _____   c. $\frac{27}{64}$ _____   d. $\frac{24}{40}$ _____   e. $\frac{21}{14}$ _____

5. Find the value of x that will give an equivalent fraction in each of the following problems.

   a. $\frac{1}{2} = \frac{x}{4}$ _____   c. $\frac{4}{5} = \frac{x}{20}$ _____   e. $\frac{3}{5} = \frac{x}{15}$ _____

   b. $\frac{6}{7} = \frac{x}{42}$ _____   d. $\frac{5}{9} = \frac{x}{63}$ _____   f. $\frac{6}{13} = \frac{42}{x}$ _____

Adding Fractions

Learning the Concept

Workers in many occupations must know how to add fractions. A plumber may have to join two pipes, one $4\frac{1}{2}$ inches long and one $5\frac{3}{4}$ inches long. To find the total length of the joined pipe, she must know how to add $4\frac{1}{2}$ inches and $5\frac{3}{4}$ inches. A pastry chef may need to know the sum of $\frac{1}{2}$ cup and $\frac{1}{3}$ cup. A mail clerk might have to find the combined weight of two packages of weight $6\frac{7}{8}$ pounds and $14\frac{1}{4}$ pounds.

Adding fractions is a bit like adding different kinds of fruit. You can add 5 apples and 6 pears if you count them all as fruit—and you make fruit salad.

Similarly, to answer the question "How much is $\frac{3}{5}$ and $\frac{2}{7}$," you make a kind of fraction salad. You can change dissimilar fractions to similar fractions by multiplying both denominators by some number that will make them alike.

$$\frac{3}{5} = \frac{?}{A} \text{ and } \frac{2}{7} = \frac{?}{A}$$

The problem is to find out what A is. In this example, you could multiply the denominator 5 in the first fraction by 7, and the denominator 7 in the second fraction by 5. Then A would be 35.

$$\frac{3}{5 \times 7} = \frac{?}{35} \quad \text{and} \quad \frac{2}{7 \times 5} = \frac{?}{35}$$

A is called the **least common denominator** (LCD) because it is the smallest (least) number that can be used for both denominators.

But remember! When you multiply one term of a fraction by some number, you *must* multiply the other term by the same number. The fractions above must be written as

$$\frac{3 \times 7}{5 \times 7} = \frac{21}{35} \quad \text{and} \quad \frac{2 \times 5}{7 \times 5} = \frac{10}{35}$$

In this form, $\frac{21}{35}$ and $\frac{10}{35}$ are similar fractions because they have the same denominator (a common denominator). Fractions with a common denominator can be added.

In order to add two similar fractions, simply add the numerators of the fractions and write the answer over the least common denominator.

$$\frac{3}{5} + \frac{2}{7} = \frac{21}{35} + \frac{10}{35} = \frac{21 + 10}{35} = \frac{31}{35}$$

The answer to this addition problem is $\frac{3}{5} + \frac{2}{7} = \frac{31}{35}$.

— Solved Examples —

EXAMPLE: What is the thickness (x) of the stub on the pin shown in Figure 2.1?

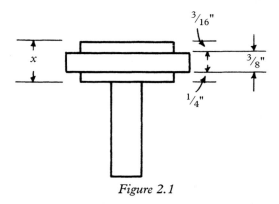

Figure 2.1

SOLUTION: The thickness of the stub of the pin x is equal to $\frac{3}{16}$" + $\frac{3}{8}$" + $\frac{1}{4}$". In this case, you have to find the LCD for three fractions. The LCD for 16, 8, and 4 is 16. Change the denominators of all three fractions to 16:

$$\frac{3}{16} = \frac{3}{16} \qquad \frac{3 \times 2}{8 \times 2} = \frac{6}{16} \qquad \frac{1 \times 4}{4 \times 4} = \frac{4}{16}$$

Now add the three fractions:

$$\frac{3}{16} + \frac{6}{16} + \frac{4}{16} = \frac{3+6+4}{16} = \frac{13}{16}$$

The stub is $\frac{13}{16}$" long. Don't forget to include the inch label!

Practice Problems

1. Add the following fractions and mixed numbers.

   a. $\frac{2}{3} + \frac{1}{4}$ _____

   b. $\frac{2}{9} + \frac{2}{5}$ _____

   c. $\frac{3}{16} + \frac{5}{8}$ _____

   d. $\frac{1}{4} + \frac{5}{12} + \frac{3}{8}$ _____

   e. $\frac{7}{8} + \frac{3}{16} + \frac{1}{64}$ _____

2. The shirt pattern on which Rosa is working calls for three pieces of cloth whose lengths are $18\frac{1}{2}$", $6\frac{1}{4}$", and $4\frac{3}{4}$". What is the total length of these three pieces?

   _____

3. Phyllis's interior design shop has been asked to wallpaper a wall divided into three sections. One section is $8\frac{1}{2}$' long, the second section is $6\frac{5}{8}$', and the third section is $15\frac{3}{4}$'. What is the total length of the wall?

   _____

4. Calculate the height of the step block shown in Figure 2.2. _____

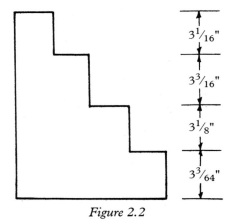

Figure 2.2

5. Find the width of the shelf bracket shown in Figure 2.3. _____

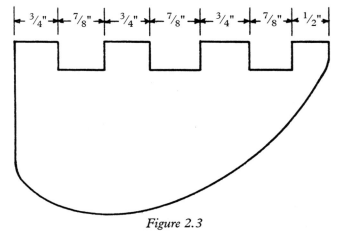

Figure 2.3

6. What is the total distance along the roof supported by the truss structure shown in Figure 2.4? (*Hint:* The two sides of the roof are of equal length.) _____

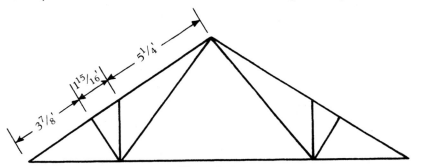

Figure 2.4

7. At the end of last month, Buddy's paving crew returned partially filled sacks of cement they had not used. Look at the records below and estimate the total amount of cement they returned.

Sack	1	2	3	4	5	6	7	8
Amount full (est.)	$\frac{1}{2}$	$\frac{1}{8}$	$\frac{4}{5}$	$\frac{3}{4}$	$\frac{1}{8}$	$\frac{2}{3}$	$\frac{1}{5}$	$\frac{1}{2}$

_____

8. The total resistance in the electrical circuit in Figure 2.5 is equal to the sum of all individual resistances. What is the total resistance, in ohms (Ω), of this circuit?

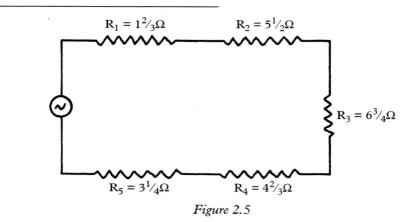

Figure 2.5

9. Vera used four pieces of #9 lead soldering wire for her last job. The four pieces were $2\frac{3}{4}$", $1\frac{5}{8}$", $21\frac{3}{16}$", and $3\frac{7}{8}$" long. What is the total length of wire she used for this job?

_____

10. What is the total length of the piercing punch shown in Figure 2.6?

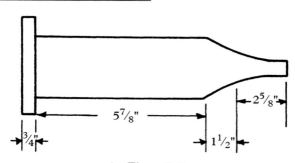

Figure 2.6

Subtracting Fractions

Learning the Concept

In many occupations you are likely to come across problems involving subtracting fractions. For example, a tool-and-die worker might have to cut a piece of metal $1\frac{3}{4}$ inches long from a piece of stock $8\frac{1}{2}$ inches long. To find out how much stock is left, the worker would have to subtract $1\frac{3}{4}$ inches from $8\frac{1}{2}$ inches. A cook may need to remove $3\frac{1}{4}$ pounds of flour from a bin that contains $12\frac{1}{4}$ pounds. She can calculate the amount of flour remaining in the bin by subtracting $3\frac{1}{4}$ pounds from $12\frac{1}{4}$ pounds. A lab technician can determine how much solution remains in a 2-liter beaker after $\frac{1}{2}$ liter has been removed by subtracting $\frac{1}{2}$ a liter from 2 liters.

The rules for subtracting fractions are similar to those for adding fractions. Before subtraction, all fractions must be changed to similar fractions with common denominators. For example, suppose you have to subtract $\frac{3}{8}$ from $\frac{15}{16}$. The first step is to find an LCD and change both fractions to similar fractions. In this case, the LCD for the two denominators—8 and 16—is 16. So,

$$\frac{3 \times 2}{8 \times 2} = \frac{6}{16} \text{ and } \frac{15}{16} = \frac{15}{16}$$

To subtract, then:

$$\frac{15}{16} - \frac{3}{8} = \frac{15}{16} - \frac{6}{16} = \frac{15-6}{16} = \frac{9}{16}$$

The answer is $\frac{9}{16}$.

— Solved Examples —

EXAMPLE: Find the width of the nail head shown in Figure 2.7.

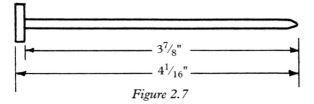

$3^7/_8$"
$4^1/_{16}$"

Figure 2.7

SOLUTION: The width of the nail head is equal to the total length of the nail ($4\frac{1}{16}$") minus the length of the shaft of the nail ($3\frac{7}{8}$"), or

$$\text{length of head} = 4\frac{1}{16}" - 3\frac{7}{8}"$$

To subtract these two you must first change the mixed numbers to improper fractions.

$$4\frac{1}{16} = \frac{65}{16}, \text{ and } 3\frac{7}{8} = \frac{31}{8}$$

Then subtract the two fractions in the usual way. The LCD for the two fractions is 16.

$$\frac{65}{16} = \frac{65}{16} \text{ and } \frac{31}{8} = \frac{31 \times 2}{8 \times 2} = \frac{62}{16}$$

Then

$$\frac{65}{16} - \frac{31}{8} = \frac{65}{16} - \frac{62}{16} = \frac{65 - 62}{16} = \frac{3}{16}$$

The width of the nail head is $\frac{3}{16}$ ".

Practice Problems

1. Perform each of the indicated subtractions.

   a. $\frac{3}{4} - \frac{1}{2}$ _____

   b. $\frac{5}{7} - \frac{1}{9}$ _____

   c. $\frac{5}{8} - \frac{1}{3}$ _____

   d. $4 - \frac{2}{3}$ _____

   e. $7\frac{7}{8} - 6\frac{1}{4}$ _____

   f. $8\frac{9}{10} - 5\frac{3}{4}$ _____

2. Ray cuts a piece of rope $3\frac{1}{4}$ feet long from a spool of rope that was originally $15\frac{3}{4}$ feet long. How much rope is left on the spool?

   _____

3. What is the thickness of the pipe shown in Figure 2.8? (*Hint:* The difference between the outer and inner diameters is twice the thickness of the pipe.)

   _____

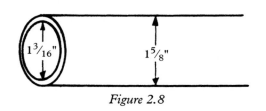

Figure 2.8

4. What is the length of the nonthreaded portion of the bolt shown in Figure 2.9?

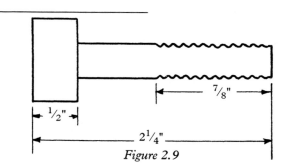

Figure 2.9

5. Mr. Xenios's lumber yard sells firewood. At the beginning of September, he had $235\frac{1}{2}$ cords of firewood in the yard. During the four weeks of September, he sold $38\frac{1}{2}$ cords, $51\frac{1}{4}$ cords, $49\frac{3}{4}$ cords, and $28\frac{1}{2}$ cords. How much wood was left at the end of September?

———————————————

6. Gail ordered aluminum sheeting $\frac{7}{8}$ " thick. The sheeting that arrived was actually $\frac{53}{64}$ " thick. Was the sheeting too thick or too thin? By how much?

———————————————

7. Use the dimensions in Figure 2.10 to calculate the diameter of the hole in the gasket.

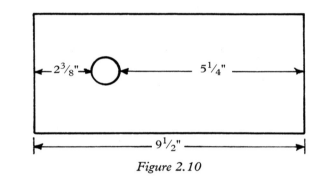

Figure 2.10

8. Calculate the length of the shaft on the drive gear shown in Figure 2.11.

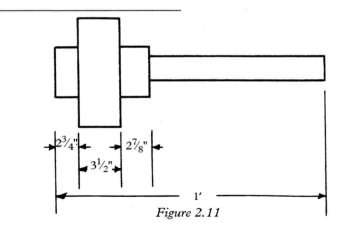

Figure 2.11

9. Edgar uses a 46-yard bolt of fabric to make four slipcovers. The amount needed for each slipcover is listed below. Indicate the amount of cloth remaining on the bolt after each slipcover has been made.

Slipcover	1	2	3	4
Amount Needed (in yards)	$10\frac{1}{2}$	$5\frac{7}{8}$	$6\frac{3}{4}$	$5\frac{3}{8}$

_____

10. Nancy has been asked to fence off a portion of the back pasture with dimensions of $128\frac{3}{4}'$ by $65\frac{7}{8}'$ by $60\frac{1}{2}'$ by $122\frac{5}{8}'$. She has 400 feet of barbed wire to work with. Does she have enough wire to make the fence? How much more will she need, or how much will be left over from her 400 feet?

_____

Multiplying Fractions

Learning the Concept

In many occupations, you may have to multiply fractions. For example, a graphic artist may need to reduce by half the size of objects in a plan he is making. That means he will have to multiply all dimensions of the object by $\frac{1}{2}$. If one dimension were $4\frac{1}{2}$ feet, he would have to multiply $4\frac{1}{2}$ by $\frac{1}{2}$.

A worker may have to multiply a whole number times a fraction. For example, a chef may want to increase a certain recipe by five times. If the original recipe calls for $1\frac{2}{3}$ cups of butter, the chef has to multiply $1\frac{2}{3}$ cups by 5.

Multiplying fractions is similar to multiplying whole numbers. For example, suppose you are asked to multiply the following two fractions:

$$\frac{1}{2} \times \frac{3}{4}$$

Simply multiply the numerators of the two fractions and the denominators of the two fractions. Then write the answer as a new fraction.

$$\frac{1}{2} \times \frac{3}{4} = \frac{1 \times 3}{2 \times 4} = \frac{3}{8}$$

To multiply mixed numbers, first change each mixed number to an improper fraction. Then multiply in the same way as above. For example, to multiply $2\frac{1}{3}$ times $3\frac{1}{4}$, first change each mixed number to an improper fraction.

$$2\frac{2}{3} = \frac{8}{3}, \text{ and } 3\frac{1}{4} = \frac{13}{4}$$

Then multiply numerator times numerator and denominator times denominator.

$$\frac{8}{3} \times \frac{13}{4} = \frac{8 \times 13}{3 \times 4} = \frac{104}{12}$$

Next, check to see that your answer is in lowest terms. Notice that your numerator and denominator can each be divided by 4.

$$\frac{104 \div 4}{12 \div 4} = \frac{26}{3}$$

Finally, change the answer back to a mixed number.

$$\frac{26}{3} = 8\frac{2}{3}$$

You can sometimes save yourself work by looking carefully at the next-to-last step in a multiplication problem. In this case, for example:

$$\frac{8 \times 13}{3 \times 4}$$

Notice that both numerator and denominator of this fraction can be divided by 4.

$$\frac{\cancel{8}2 \times 13}{3 \times \cancel{4}1}$$

Multiplying now gives you a fraction already in its lowest terms.

— Solved Examples —

EXAMPLE: All six seamstresses at Joanna's will need $8\frac{2}{3}$ yards of fabric to make the dresses they are working on. What is the total yardage of material Joanna will need to order?

SOLUTION: The total yardage is found by multiplying the number of workers times the number of yards needed by each worker.

$$6 \times 8\frac{2}{3}$$

To do this multiplication, change the mixed number to an improper fraction. Write the whole number as a fraction whose denominator is 1.

$$6 \times 8\frac{2}{3} = \frac{6}{1} \times \frac{26}{3} = \frac{6 \times 26}{1 \times 3}$$

Both the numerator and denominator of the last fraction can be divided by 3. After doing so, multiply the fraction as usual.

$$\frac{\cancel{6}2 \times 26}{1 \times \cancel{3}1} = 52 \text{ yards}$$

Practice Problems

1. Perform these multiplications.

   a. $\frac{2}{3} \times \frac{1}{5}$ _____

   b. $\frac{4}{5} \times \frac{3}{8}$ _____

   c. $\frac{2}{9} \times \frac{1}{4} \times \frac{3}{8}$ _____

   d. $12 \times \frac{5}{6}$ _____

   e. $5\frac{3}{4} \times 2\frac{7}{8}$ _____

   f. $3\frac{9}{16} \times 2\frac{2}{3}$ _____

2. Chun will need 8 boards, each $9\frac{1}{4}$ feet long, for the bookcase he is building. What is the total length of the lumber he needs for the bookcase?

   _____

3. The contents of each full cask of wine at a winery weigh $58\frac{3}{4}$ pounds. What is the weight of half the contents? Three-quarters? One-ninth?

   _____

4. Each bundle of shingles used by Kermit in his roofing business weighs $35\frac{1}{2}$ pounds. What is the total weight of $15\frac{1}{2}$ of these bundles?

   _____

5. Lila's catering service has to adjust recipes to serve large numbers of people. What quantities would she have to use to serve 36 people if the recipe she has is for 8 people? The ingredients for the 8-person recipe are as follows:

   $2\frac{1}{3}$ cups flour _____ $1\frac{3}{4}$ cups sugar _____

   3 tsp vanilla extract _____ $\frac{3}{8}$ cup nuts _____

   2 tsp baking soda _____   2 eggs _____

   $\frac{1}{4}$ cup raisins _____

   (*Hint:* Multiply each measurement by 36/8.)

6. A bag of almonds from Vera's grove weighs $56\frac{3}{4}$ pounds. What is the weight of $2\frac{2}{3}$ bags of nuts?

   _____

7. Tri needs 300 pounds of fertilizer to finish covering his cornfield. He has $3\frac{1}{4}$ bags of fertilizer, each weighing $85\frac{1}{2}$ pounds when full. How many pounds of fertilizer does he have in all? By how much is he short, or by how much is he over?

   _____

8. In cleaning up after his latest job, Kevin finds that he has four bags of plaster left over. One bag is about an eighth full, one about a third full, one three-quarters full, and one about seven-eighths full. Estimate how many bags of plaster are left over. A full bag of plaster weighs $36\frac{1}{2}$ pounds. About what weight of plaster does Kevin have left?

   _____

9. A spool of aluminum wire weighs $\frac{1}{2}$ ounce per running foot. What is the weight in pounds of aluminum on a spool holding 20 yards of wire?

   _____

10. An average-size peck of walnuts weighs $14\frac{7}{16}$ pounds. Use the chart below to determine how many pounds of walnuts each picker turned in last week.

Pecks Turned In

Picker	Monday	Tuesday	Wednesday	Thursday	Friday
Tom	—	$8\frac{1}{2}$	$8\frac{1}{4}$	$9\frac{3}{4}$	$9\frac{1}{4}$
Mikhail	$10\frac{1}{2}$	—	—	$12\frac{1}{4}$	$12\frac{1}{2}$
Turi	—	$7\frac{1}{2}$	$14\frac{1}{2}$	$9\frac{1}{2}$	—

Tom: _____

Mikhail: _____

Turi: _____

Dividing Fractions

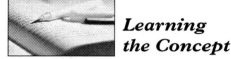

*Learning
the Concept*

Dividing fractions and whole numbers is a skill you may need in some occupations. To divide $35\frac{1}{2}$ gallons of paint among four workers, a painter has to know how to divide $35\frac{1}{2}$ by 4. A carpenter may want to cut a board $12\frac{3}{4}$ feet long into 5 equal parts. To know how long each part must be, the carpenter should be able to divide $12\frac{3}{4}$ by 5.

The rule for dividing fractions is: Invert the divisor and multiply. Once you know how to invert the divisor, dividing fractions is the same as multiplying fractions.

In the problem $\frac{2}{3} \div \frac{3}{4}$, the fraction that follows the division sign ($\frac{3}{4}$) is the *divisor*. The word *invert* means to "turn upside down." When you invert the fraction $\frac{3}{4}$, you get the fraction $\frac{4}{3}$. So, the way to solve the problem $\frac{2}{3} \div \frac{3}{4}$ is to change its format, as follows:

$$\frac{2}{3} \div \frac{3}{4} = \frac{2}{3} \times \frac{4}{3}$$

Now you have a multiplication problem that you know how to do:

$$\frac{2}{3} \times \frac{4}{3} = \frac{8}{9}$$

— Solved Examples —

EXAMPLE: An electrician has $25\frac{1}{2}$ feet of wire. How many pieces $2\frac{1}{4}$ feet long can she cut from the wire?

SOLUTION: The problem is to find out how many times $25\frac{1}{2}$ feet can be divided by $2\frac{1}{4}$ feet. Write the problem this way.

$$25\frac{1}{2} \div 2\frac{1}{4}$$

Change both mixed numbers to improper fractions, and follow the rule for dividing fractions.

$$25\frac{1}{2} = \frac{51}{2} \text{ and } 2\frac{1}{4} = \frac{9}{4} = \frac{\overset{17}{\cancel{51}} \times \overset{2}{\cancel{4}}}{\underset{1}{\cancel{2}} \times \underset{3}{\cancel{9}}} = \frac{34}{3} = 11\frac{1}{3}$$

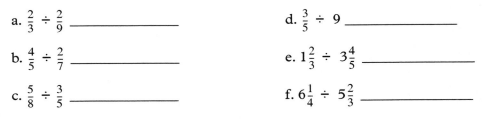

Practice Problems

1. Perform each of the indicated divisions.

   a. $\frac{2}{3} \div \frac{2}{9}$ _____

   b. $\frac{4}{5} \div \frac{2}{7}$ _____

   c. $\frac{5}{8} \div \frac{3}{5}$ _____

   d. $\frac{3}{5} \div 9$ _____

   e. $1\frac{2}{3} \div 3\frac{4}{5}$ _____

   f. $6\frac{1}{4} \div 5\frac{2}{3}$ _____

2. David needs $12\frac{2}{3}$ feet of electrical wire to wind a solenoid. How many solenoids can he wind with 200 feet of wire?

   _____

3. Eric wants to saw boards that are 2 feet 4 inches long from a piece of stock 25 feet long. How many boards will he get from the stock?

   _____

4. Mona plans to hang three custom-fitted shades on a window that is $14\frac{3}{4}$' wide. What will be the width of each shade?

   _____

5. The holes in the template in Figure 2.12 are equally spaced. How far apart are they?

   _____

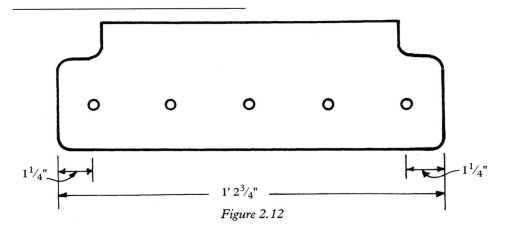

$1\frac{1}{4}$" $1\frac{1}{4}$"

$1'\ 2\frac{3}{4}$"

Figure 2.12

6. Mary plans to floor a room 20 feet 4 inches wide with boards that are $4\frac{3}{4}$" wide. How many boards will she need to cover the width of the floor?

   _____

7. In Mason's plant, soup is transported from a cooking vat to the canning machine in pipes of various sizes. Tell how long it would take to fill 100 of each size can listed below from the pipe indicated.

Volume of Can (oz)	$2\frac{1}{8}$	$4\frac{1}{4}$	$6\frac{1}{2}$	$9\frac{3}{4}$	12
Pipe Flow (oz per min)	$4\frac{1}{4}$	$6\frac{1}{2}$	9	$11\frac{7}{16}$	$15\frac{2}{3}$

8. From the dimensions on the floor plan in Figure 2.13, calculate the actual dimensions of the space. The scale is 1 inch to 4 feet.

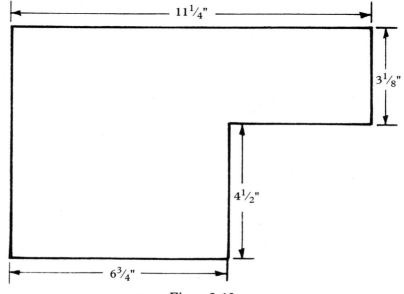

Figure 2.13

DECIMALS AND PERCENTS

Decimals and Percents

Learning the Concept

Any common fraction with a denominator of 10, 100, 1,000, or some other multiple of 10 can also be expressed as a decimal. A *decimal* is a number that contains a decimal point. The numbers below are all decimals.

0.3   0.45   0.879

The zero (0) in each of the decimals above is often added for the sake of clarity, to help keep the decimal point from getting lost in text or in a report, a table, a chart, or a problem.

The mixed numbers below contain a whole-number part (the part to the left of the decimal point) and a decimal part (the part to the right of the decimal point).

3.4   8.79   152.438

Each position in a decimal stands for a fraction whose denominator is 10, 100, 1,000, 10,000, and so on. (To review, read pages 1-3 in Chapter 1.) The number 0.349758 illustrates this point. The value of each digit in this number is illustrated in Figure 3.1:

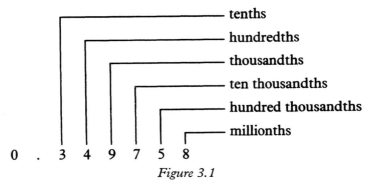

Figure 3.1

The digit 3 in the above number means $\frac{3}{10}$, or 0.3.

The digit 4 means $\frac{4}{100}$, or 0.04.

The digit 9 means $\frac{9}{1,000}$, or 0.009.

The digit 7 means $\frac{7}{10,000}$, or 0.000 7.

The digit 5 means $\frac{5}{100,000}$, or 0.000 05.

The digit 8 means $\frac{8}{1,000,000}$, or 0.000 008.

The number 0.349758 means 0.3 + 0.04 + 0.009 + 0.000 7 + 0.000 05 + 0.000 008.

Digits to the right of the decimal point are arranged in groups of three to make the number easier to read and understand.

Numbers that contain less than a whole can be expressed either as fractions or decimals. Fractions are often used in the British system of measurement (for example, feet, inches, pounds, quarts, etc.). Decimals are used in the metric system (for example, meters, liters, grams, etc.). Most calculators use only decimals to represent numbers that are less than a whole.

The first skill to learn in working with fractions and decimals is how to change from one system to the other. For example, you may have to change the decimal 0.519 to a fraction. Or you may have to change the fraction $\frac{3}{8}$ to a decimal.

You can change a decimal to a fraction simply by reading the number. For example, read the decimal 0.519 as "five hundred nineteen thousandths." The fraction equivalent to the decimal 0.519 has a numerator of 519 and a denominator of 1,000. So the decimal 0.519 is equivalent to the fraction $\frac{519}{1,000}$.

To change a fraction to a decimal, just remember that the line separating numerator and denominator means *divided by*. So the fraction $\frac{3}{4}$ means 3 *divided by* 4. When you carry out that division, you find that 3 *divided by* 4 is equal to 0.75.

$$
\begin{array}{r}
.\,7\ 5 \\
4\,\overline{)\,3\,.\,0\ 0} \\
2\quad 8 \\
\hline
2\ 0 \\
2\ 0 \\
\hline
\end{array}
$$

Percents are a special kind of decimal. A number expressed as a percent is really a fraction with 100 as the denominator. The following numbers can all be expressed directly as percents because they are decimals whose last digit is in the hundredths place:

0.94   0.16   0.05

The word *percent* means hundredths. When you write a number with a percent sign (%), you express the number as parts of a hundred; that is, you express the number as hundredths.

$$0.94 = \frac{94}{100} = 94\% \qquad 0.16 = \frac{16}{100} = 16\% \qquad 0.05 = \frac{5}{100} = 5\%$$

Of course, the reverse is true, too. The expression 47% means 47 hundredths, or 0.47, or $\frac{47}{100}$.

Now we can state the rules for converting decimals to and from percents:

To change a decimal to a percent, move the decimal point two places to the right and add a percent sign.

For example, to change the number 0.485 to a percent, move the decimal point two places to the right:

$$0.485 \quad = \quad 48.5$$

and add a percent sign: 48.5%

Thus, 0.485 = 48.5%.

To change a number from a percent to a decimal, move the decimal point two places to the left and remove the percent sign.

For example, to change 39.805% to a decimal, move the decimal point two places to the left:

$$39.805\% \quad = \quad 0.39805\%$$

and remove the percent sign: 0.39805

Common fractions, decimals, and percents are closely related. The diagram below shows that any one kind of fraction can be changed into any other kind of fraction.

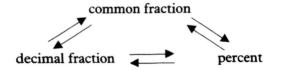

The following Solved Examples and Practice Problems show how to make these conversions.

— Solved Examples —

EXAMPLE A: Change the decimal 0.8571 to its equivalent as a common fraction.

SOLUTION: Read the decimal to yourself: "Eight thousand, five hundred seventy-one ten thousandths." That tells you that the numerator is 8,571 and the denominator is 10,000. Write: $\frac{8,571}{10,000}$. Thus, $0.8571 = \frac{8,571}{10,000}$.

EXAMPLE B: Write the common fraction $\frac{11}{15}$ as a decimal. Round off the answer to the hundredths place.

SOLUTION: Perform the division indicated by the fraction line in $\frac{11}{15}$:

```
              .  7  3  3
      1  5 | 1  1  .  0  0  0  0
              1  0     5
                       5  0
                       4  5
                          5  0
                          4  5
                             5
```

The answer is 0.733 . . . where the . . . (ellipses) mean that you do not get an exact answer. You can go on dividing forever. An answer like this is sometimes called a *repeating decimal*.

The instructions above say to round off the answer to the hundredths place. The term *round off* means to decide what the last number in your answer will be. In this case, you decide your last number will be in the hundredths place. Your answer must be in the form 0.X X.

To round off to the hundredths place, begin by looking at the first digit after the hundredths place. If that number is 5 or greater, increase the hundredths place by 1. Because 9 is greater than 5, for example, 0.579 rounded off to the hundredths place is 0.58.

If that number is less than 5, keep the digit in the hundredths place and drop all the following digits. Because 1 is less than 5, for example, 0.461 rounded to the hundredths place is 0.46.

In the answer to Example B above (0.733 . . .), the digit following the hundredths place is 3. Rounded off to the hundredths place, the number becomes 0.73.

Practice Problems

1. Change the following common fractions to decimals.

    a. $\frac{7}{10}$ _____

    b. $\frac{237}{1,000}$ _____

    c. $\frac{1}{4}$ _____

    d. $\frac{3}{16}$ _____

    e. $\frac{13}{50}$ _____

    f. $\frac{3}{7}$ _____

Round off answer to the ten thousandths place.

2. Change the following decimals to common fractions in their lowest terms.

    a. 0.7 _____

    b. 0.95 _____

    c. 0.25 _____

    d. 0.007 _____

    e. 0.139 _____

    f. 0.46 _____

3. Change the following common fractions to whole percents.

   a. $\frac{7}{8}$ _____   d. $\frac{5}{6}$ _____

   b. $\frac{4}{5}$ _____   e. $\frac{1}{3}$ _____

   c. $\frac{1}{7}$ _____   f. $\frac{7}{15}$ _____

4. Change the following decimals to whole percents.

   a. 0.29 _____   d. 0.895 _____

   b. 0.06 _____   e. 0.778 _____

   c. 0.99 _____   f. 0.054 _____

5. Change the following percents to decimals.

   a. 32% _____   d. 46.5% _____

   b. 66% _____   e. 89.1% _____

   c. 75% _____   f. 17.86% _____

6. Change the following percents to common fractions in their lowest terms.

   a. 25% _____   d. 62.5% _____

   b. 8% _____   e. 63.7% _____

   c. 42% _____   f. 14.7% _____

Adding Decimals

*Learning
the Concept*

Adding decimals is a common operation in the workplace. For example, a lab technician might need to know the total volume of three solutions whose individual volumes are 6.9 mL, 1.8 mL, and 3.5 mL. She could find the answer by adding 6.9 mL + 1.8 mL + 3.5 mL. A carpenter might have to find the total length of two boards that measure 2.4 meters and 4.0 meters. He can add 2.4 meters + 4.0 meters.

All money calculations involve decimals. To figure a bill, for example, a clerk has to add decimals. She might have to find the sum of $5.81, $18.95, and $23.86. That kind of problem requires the addition of decimals.

Adding decimals requires the same skills you use to add whole numbers. But you do have to keep one very special caution in mind. Before you add decimals, make sure that the numbers are properly arranged. Make sure that the decimal points are in a vertical column.

For example, to add the numbers 0.132 + 0.251 + 0.316, set up

$$
\begin{array}{r}
0.1\ 3\ 2 \\
+\ 0.2\ 5\ 1 \\
+\ 0.3\ 1\ 6 \\
\hline
\end{array}
$$

Notice that the decimal points are aligned exactly above and below each other. By arranging the decimal points properly, you will be certain that all the tenths in every number, all the hundredths, all the thousandths, and so on, will be lined up. If you do not set up the problem carefully, you can end up adding the tenths digit in one number to the hundredths digit in a second number and the units digit in a third number. Then your answer will have no meaning at all.

Once you have the problem set up properly, simply add the numbers as if they were whole numbers. But don't forget to keep track of where the decimal point belongs in the answer!

$$
\begin{array}{r}
0.1\ 3\ 2 \\
+\ 0.2\ 5\ 1 \\
+\ 0.3\ 1\ 6 \\
\hline
0.6\ 9\ 9
\end{array}
$$

You can use a calculator to add decimals, just as you did with whole numbers. The calculator will keep track of the decimal point for you.

— Solved Examples —

EXAMPLE A: Add 2.58 + 3.164 + 7.55. Round off your answer to the hundredths place.

SOLUTION: First, set up the problem correctly, with the decimal points aligned.

$$
\begin{array}{r}
2\ .\ 5\ 8 \\
+\ 3\ .\ 1\ 6\ 4 \\
+\ 7\ .\ 5\ 5 \\
\hline
\end{array}
$$

Proceed by adding columns from right to left, carrying where necessary.

$$
\begin{array}{r}
{}^{1}2\ .\ {}^{1}5\ 8 \\
+\ 3\ .\ 1\ 6\ 4 \\
+\ 7\ .\ 5\ 5 \\
\hline
1\ 3\ .\ 2\ 9\ 4
\end{array}
$$

Finally, to round off to the hundredths place, notice that the digit following the hundredths place (4) is less than 5. So, by the rules of rounding, you should just drop that digit and keep a 9 in the hundredths place. The final answer is 13.29.

EXAMPLE B: Use a calculator to add 2.37 + 4.29 + 8.87.

SOLUTION:

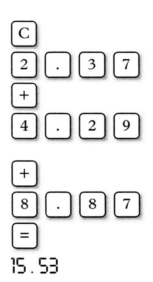

1. Clear display.

2. Enter any one of the numbers.

3. Press the addition key.

4. Enter either of the two remaining numbers.

5. Press the addition key.

6. Enter the third number.

7. Press the equals key.

8. Read the answer on the display.

Practice Problems

1. Perform each of the indicated additions.

a.
$$
\begin{array}{r}
0\ .\ 4\ 1 \\
+\ 0\ .\ 3\ 2 \\
\hline
\end{array}
$$

b.
$$
\begin{array}{r}
0\ .\ 6\ 3\ 1 \\
+\ 0\ .\ 2\ 6\ 5 \\
\hline
\end{array}
$$

c.
$$
\begin{array}{r}
0\ .\ 4\ 8 \\
+\ 0\ .\ 3\ 9 \\
\hline
\end{array}
$$

d.   0 . 2 5
    + 0 . 3 7 9
    _____
    _____

e.   0 . 4 3 2
    + 0 . 1 6 3
    + 0 . 3 0 4
    _____
    _____

f.   0 . 5 1 6
    + 0 . 4 3
    + 0 . 8 9 5
    _____
    _____

g. 1.382 + 3.562 + 0.179 _____

h. 1.47 + 3.67 _____

i. 5.662 + 4.358 _____

j. 11.82 + 5.677 + 4.9 _____

2. Round off each of the following numbers to the nearest tenth.

a. 5.62 _____   b. 0.47 _____   c. 9.25 _____   d. 17.47 _____

3. Round off each of the following numbers to the nearest hundredth:

a. 0.481 _____   b. 0.527 _____   c. 4.855 _____   d. 15.62 _____

4. Renee makes a saline solution by adding 55.3 mL of water to 2.4 mL of a sodium chloride solution. What is the total volume of this solution?

_____

5. A piece of plywood consists of five layers of the following thicknesses: 0.150 in, 0.325 in, 0.500 in, 0.325 in, and 0.150 in. What is the total thickness of the plywood?

_____

6. What is the total width of the gasket shown in Figure 3.2, to the nearest tenth of an inch?

_____

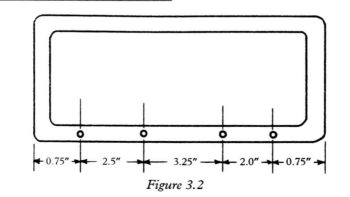

0.75"   2.5"   3.25"   2.0"   0.75"

Figure 3.2

7. Myra uses slugs of four widths in a print job. The widths of the slugs are as follows: 0.75", 1.35", 1.78", and 2.07". What is the total width of the four slugs together?

    _____

8. The circuit Lydia has designed for a new transistor has the shape shown in Figure 3.3. What is the total length of the circuit? The length of each segment in the circuit is as follows:

    AB = 0.015"   EF = 0.032"

    BC = 0.012"   FG = 0.0076"

    CD = 0.022"   GH = 0.0053"

    DE = 0.0026"   HA = 0.0070"

    _____

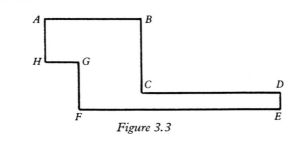

Figure 3.3

9. What is the total length of the nozzle shown in Figure 3.4?

    _____

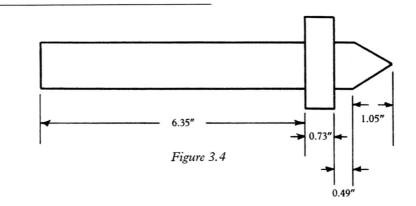

Figure 3.4

10. Calculate the exact length of the probe shown in Figure 3.5.

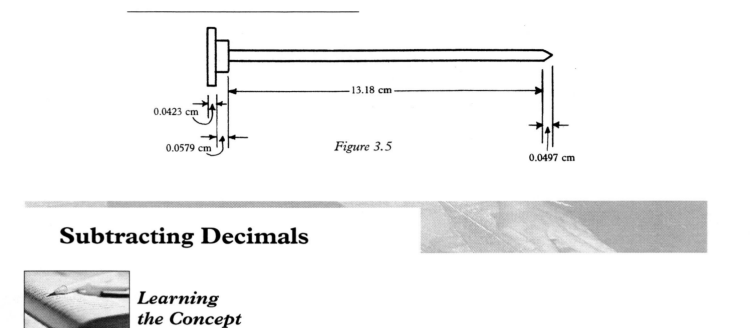

0.0423 cm

0.0579 cm

13.18 cm

0.0497 cm

Figure 3.5

Subtracting Decimals

Learning the Concept

Knowing how to subtract decimals is important in most occupations. A lathe operator might have to remove 0.9 inch from a 45.7-inch steel rod. She could find the final length of the rod by subtracting 0.9 inch from 45.7 inches. A bookkeeper may want to know how much remains in an account after writing a check for $87.52 if the balance in the account before he writes the check is $1,057.14. A high school student may want to calculate how much is left to reach the $5,000.00 goal of a fund drive if $3,968.87 has already been collected.

You can subtract decimals as easily as you can subtract whole numbers if you remember one warning: Always be sure to align the numbers to be subtracted, just as you do when you add decimals.

For example, suppose you want to subtract 1.73 cm from 3.48 cm. The first step is to align the decimal points and digits in a vertical column.

$$
\begin{array}{r}
3\ .\ 4\ 8 \\
-\ 1\ .\ 7\ 3 \\
\hline
\end{array}
$$

Then, subtract as you would with whole numbers, remembering to align the decimal point in your answer.

$$
\begin{array}{r}
3\ .\ 4\ 8 \\
-\ 1\ .\ 7\ 3 \\
\hline
1\ .\ 7\ 5 \\
\end{array}
$$

You can use a calculator to subtract decimal numbers. The calculator keeps track of the decimal point for you.

EXAMPLE A: Vera withdraws 10.47 mL from a flask originally containing 25.39 mL of solution. How much solution remains in the flask?

SOLUTION: The problem is to subtract 10.47 mL from 25.39 mL. Align the numbers, with the decimal point in the proper place in the answer, and subtract as you do with whole numbers.

$$
\begin{array}{r}
2\ 5\ .\ 3\ 9 \quad \text{mL} \\
-\ 1\ 0\ .\ 4\ 7 \quad \text{mL} \\
\hline
1\ 4\ .\ 9\ 2 \quad \text{mL}
\end{array}
$$

EXAMPLE B: Subtract 5.839 from 10.126 using a calculator.

SOLUTION:

1. Clear display.

2. Enter the minuend.

3. Press the subtraction key.

4. Enter the subtrahend.

5. Press the equals key.

6. Read the answer on the display.

| C |

| 1 | 0 | . | 1 | 2 | 6 |

| − |

| 5 | . | 8 | 3 | 9 |

| = |

4.287

Practice Problems

1. Carry out the following subtraction problems. (*Hint:* For problem f, change 9 to 9.000 before you subtract.)

a.
$$
\begin{array}{r}
0\ .\ 9\ 5 \\
-\ 0\ .\ 6\ 2 \\
\hline
\end{array}
$$

b.
$$
\begin{array}{r}
1\ 6\ .\ 8\ 6 \\
-\ 1\ 5\ .\ 4\ 7 \\
\hline
\end{array}
$$

c.
$$
\begin{array}{r}
1\ .\ 8\ 2\ 3 \\
-\ 0\ .\ 1\ 6\ 5 \\
\hline
\end{array}
$$

d. 10.047 − 5.823 _____

e. 16.641 − 8.878 _____

f. 9 − 6.425 _____

2. What is the width of the opening in the gasket shown in Figure 3.6? (*Hint:* Subtract the width of both left and right edges from the total width of the gasket. Assume the edges are of equal width.)

_____

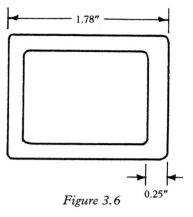

Figure 3.6   0.25"

3. Joshua cuts a piece of pipe 12.6" long from a piece of stock that is 100" long. How much pipe remains on this stock?

_____

4. Gerard's print shop is making a mat that will print in light, normal, and bold shades. Bold letters are to be raised 0.45" above the mat, normal letters 0.090" below that, and light letters 0.075" below that. How high are the normal and light letters above the mat?

_____

5. What is the size of each dimension marked x in the part shown in Figure 3.7? Assume that x is the same width in both cases.

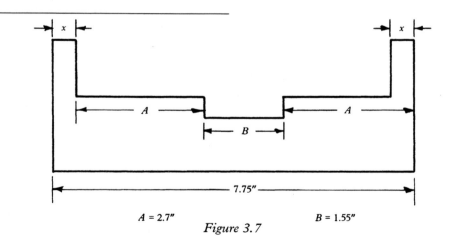

A = 2.7"   B = 1.55"

Figure 3.7

6. An iron rod delivered to Joy's machine shop has a diameter of 3". The rod must have a finished diameter of 2.795". She turns the rod down by 0.142" on her lathe. Has she reduced the diameter to the 2.795" diameter required? If not, by how much more must the rod be reduced?

_____

7. Soo Mae measures the amount of fuel oil she delivers to a customer by measuring the volume of oil in her truck before delivery and then after delivery. Calculate the amount of fuel oil delivered at each of the stops shown in the chart below. Round off all answers to the nearest tenth of a gallon.

Stop	Volume of Oil before Delivery (gallons)	Volume of Oil after Delivery (gallons)
221 Bemis	3,046	2,796.65
248 Bemis	2,796.65	2,567.40
296 Bemis	2,567.40	2,368.55
235 Evenson	2,368.55	2,129.75
388 Evenson	2,129.75	1,916.20

_____

8. A piece of silver wire 0.085" thick is to be used as a piece of microcircuitry. The wire is originally 6.000" long. How much remains after pieces of the following lengths are cut?

Piece 1: 1.550" _____   Piece 3: 0.7595" _____

Piece 2: 0.5875" _____   Piece 4: 0.08875" _____

9. Sonia's work as a medical technologist requires her to make solutions. The usual procedure is to add distilled water to a stock solution to produce a desired concentration. Use the following table to determine how much water to add to the stock solution to prepare the final volume of solution.

Final Volume (in ML)	100.0	100.0	63.6	50.00	35.75	1.053
Stock Solution (in ML)	7.5	13.75	8.9	0.75	8.89	0.268

_____

10. Nate uses sheets of galvanized metal of five thicknesses in his work. Calculate how much thicker each sheet is than the next thinner sheet from the chart below.

Gauge Number	7	8	9	10	11
Thickness (in inches)	0.1793	0.1644	0.1494	0.1345	0.1196

_____

Multiplying Decimals

Learning the Concept

Workers are often required to multiply decimals. For example, Yvonne may have to determine the paycheck for someone who has worked 35.75 hours at a pay rate of $11.79 per hour. To make that calculation, she would have to multiply 35.75 hours times $11.79 per hour. An electrician multiplies current times voltage to find the power output in a circuit. A graphic artist might have to increase the dimensions of a drawing 2.5 times.

If you can multiply whole numbers, you can multiply decimals. You have to learn only one new skill: where to place the decimal point in the answer. For example, suppose you are asked to multiply 2.32 by 1.2. Set up the problem as you would any whole-number multiplication problem.

$$\begin{array}{r} 2 \ . \ 3 \ 2 \\ \times \quad 1 \ . \ 2 \\ \hline \end{array}$$

Then, go ahead and multiply. (Ignore the decimal points for the moment.)

$$\begin{array}{r} 2 \ . \ 3 \ 2 \\ \times \quad 1 \ . \ 2 \\ \hline 4 \quad 6 \ 4 \\ 2 \ 3 \quad 2 \quad \\ \hline 2 \ 7 \quad 8 \ 4 \end{array}$$

Now, to locate the decimal point in the answer, count the total number of decimal places in the two numbers you have just multiplied.

2 . 3 2 has two decimal places (2 . 3 2)

1 . 2 has one decimal place (1 . 2)

That makes a total of three decimal places (2 + 1 = 3) in the two numbers you have just multiplied. So three will be the number of decimal places in your answer. Start at the right-hand end of your answer and count over to the left until you have three decimal places.

2 . 7 8 4

2 . 7 8 4

The answer to the multiplication problem 2.32 × 1.2 is 2.784.

— Solved Examples —

EXAMPLE A: Andrea wants to find the weight of 24.5 mL of ethyl alcohol. One milliliter (mL) of ethyl alcohol weighs 0.78 grams (0.78 g).

SOLUTION: Multiply the weight of one milliliter of ethyl alcohol (0.78 g) by 24.5 mL.

$$
\begin{array}{r}
2\ 4.\ 5 \ \text{mL} \\
\times \quad 0.\ 7\ 8 \ \text{g/mL} \\
\hline
1\ 9\ 6\ 0 \\
1\ 7\ 1\ 5 \quad\ \\
\hline
1\ 9\ 1\ 1\ 0 \\
\end{array}
$$

The first number you are multiplying contains one decimal place (24.5 mL); the second number contains two decimal places (0.78 g/mL). After adding those decimal places (2 + 1 = 3), you know your answer must contain three decimal places: 19.110 g.

EXAMPLE B: Use a calculator to multiply 3.82 times 8.71.

SOLUTION:

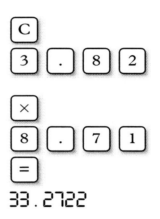

1. Clear display.

2. Enter either of the numbers to be multiplied.

3. Press the multiplication key.

4. Enter the second number.

5. Press the equals key.

6. Read the answer on the display.

Notice that the calculator gives the complete correct answer with the decimal point in the correct place.

Practice Problems

1. Perform each of the indicated multiplications.

a.
$$
\begin{array}{r}
0\ .\ 3 \\
\times\ 0\ .\ 2 \\
\hline
\end{array}
$$

b.
$$
\begin{array}{r}
1\ .\ 4\ 3 \\
\times\quad 0\ .\ 6 \\
\hline
\end{array}
$$

c.
$$
\begin{array}{r}
1\ 5\ .\ 8 \\
\times\quad 4\ .\ 7 \\
\hline
\end{array}
$$

d. 0.32 × 7 _____

e. 4.65 × 7.12 _____

f. 250×4.8 _____

g. 30.6×4.58 _____

h. $14.3 \times 28 \times 1.62$ _____

2. Mason's hourly pay as a plumber's apprentice is $13.75 per hour. What would his paycheck be for a 7-hour day? For a 35-hour week?

_____

3. For a project submitted to her commercial-art firm, Bev has to increase the dimensions of a sketch 2.75 times. Find each of the final dimensions, if the original dimensions are as follows:

AB = 4.0 in _____   DE = 1.25 in _____

BC = 2.5 in _____   EF = 5.75 in _____

CD = 3.5 in _____   FA = 4.75 in _____

4. The waterbeds Myron sells have an average size of 22.5 cubic feet. One cubic foot of water weighs 62.4 pounds. What is the weight of one waterbed? What is the total weight of the 15 waterbeds Myron now has on display in his store?

_____

5. Sam has ordered three kinds of brass bolts: 400 of type A, 550 of type B, and 675 of type C. The weight of each bolt is listed below. What is the total weight of each kind of bolt and the total weight of the order?

Bolt Type	A	B	C
Weight per Bolt (oz)	0.96	1.36	1.91

_____

6. A machine stamps out 250 bushings of the shape shown in Figure 3.8 in one minute. How fast does stock have to be fed into the machine to maintain this rate of production?

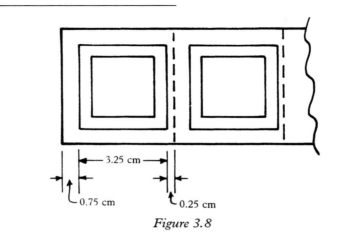

3.25 cm

0.75 cm

0.25 cm

Figure 3.8

7. In Tom's plant, a milling machine can deliver aluminum sheeting at various speeds. What length of sheeting will be delivered per hour for each of these settings?

Setting	1	2	3	4	5
Speed (feet/minute)	3.5	5.75	10.25	32.5	125.75

8. The largest saw in Rhea's mill can be set to cut lumber at various speeds. How much lumber can be cut in one 8-hour day for each of the following settings?

Setting	1	2	3	4
Speed (feet/minute)	2.5	6.8	8.75	10.95

9. Chin is putting down new flooring made of boards of three different widths. He is using 20 boards 4.8 cm wide, 35 boards 5.7 cm wide, and 8 boards 4.9 cm wide. What is the total width of the floor Chin installs?

Dividing Decimals

*Learning
the Concept*

An office manager may have to divide a bonus of $750.00 equally among six employees. To find how much each employee should receive, the manager divides $750.00 by 6. A lab technician might want to know how many bottles, each holding 12.5 mL, can be filled from a 500 mL container. She could find out by dividing 500 mL by 12.5 mL.

Dividing decimals is similar to dividing whole numbers. Just as it is with multiplication, the issue is knowing where to put the decimal point in the answer. Consider the problem in the following example: Divide 2.34 by 1.3.

First, write the problem in the proper division format.

$$1\;.\;3\,\overline{\big)\,2\;.\;3\;4}$$

Next, move the decimal point in the divisor all the way to the right, to make the divisor a whole number.

$$1\;.\;3\,\overline{\big)\,2\;.\;3\;4}$$

Count the number of places you have moved the decimal point. In this example, you moved the decimal point one place. Now move the decimal point in the dividend the same number of places (in this example, one place).

$$1\;3\;.\,\overline{\big)\,2\;.\;3\;4}$$

Put the decimal point in your answer directly above the decimal point in the dividend.

$$1\;3\;.\,\overline{\big)\,2\;.\;3\;4}$$

Now, go ahead and divide, as you would with whole numbers. Make sure to keep the decimal point in your answer in its proper place.

$$
1\;3\;.\,\overline{\big)\!\begin{array}{r} 1\;. \\ 2\;3\;.\;4 \\ \underline{1\;3} \\ 1\;0 \end{array}}
$$

and

```
            1 . 8
  1 3 . | 2 3 . 4
          1 3
          ‾‾‾‾‾
          1 0   4
          1 0   4
          ‾‾‾‾‾
```

Answer: 2.34 divided by 1.3 is 1.8.

— Solved Examples —

EXAMPLE: Wes wants to calculate the average speed for his last trip. He traveled 504.6 miles in 11.6 hours. Use a calculator to solve this problem.

SOLUTION: Wes can solve this problem by dividing the distance he traveled (504.6 miles) by the time it took to drive that distance (11.6 hours).

1. Clear display.
   [C]

2. Enter dividend.
   [5] [0] [4] [.] [6]

3. Press division key.
   [÷]

4. Enter divisor.
   [1] [1] [.] [6]

5. Press the equals key.
   [=]

6. Read the answer on the display.
   43.5

Wes drove at an average speed of 43.5 miles per hour on the trip.

Practice Problems

1. Perform each of the following indicated divisions. For problems that do not come out evenly, round off your answer to the nearest hundredth.

   a. 42 | 235.2

   b. 2.3 | 13.11

   c. 4.7 | 5.83

   d. 14.3 ÷ 1.7

   e. 25 ÷ 1.75

   f. 0.895 ÷ 0.15

   g. 1.325 ÷ 25.5

   h. 0.5 ÷ 6.7

   i. 15.675 ÷ 125.5

2. How many pieces of wallpaper, each 2.75 feet wide, will Dennis need in order to cover a wall that is 15 feet wide?

3. The IV that Marlene has placed into a patient's arm releases 2.5 mL of solution per minute. How long will the IV have to remain in position to release a total of 300 mL of solution?

4. A pile of sheet metal 62.5 cm high consists of sheets that are 0.1475 cm thick. How many sheets are there in the pile?

5. A piece of copper wire 20.75 meters long is cut into 18.5 cm lengths. How many pieces of wire can be cut from this stock? (1 meter = 100 cm)

6. The threads on the bolt in Figure 3.9 are 0.176" wide. How many threads are there in the bolt if the threaded portion is 3.168" long?

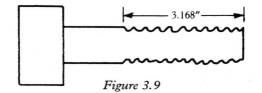

Figure 3.9

7. The pins shown in Figure 3.10 are stamped out of stock that is 50 feet long. The dimensions of the pin are given. The waste at each end of the pin totals 0.073". How many pins can be stamped from the available stock?

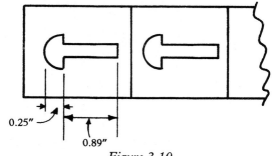

Figure 3.10

8. Oscar's job is to lay down successive layers of an aluminum film on a glass background that will serve as the base of a new telescope. What is the minimum number of layers needed if the total thickness of the film is to be 0.4325 cm, and each layer is 0.00017 cm thick?

9. Paul's government grant for $47,239.92 allows him to pay his workers $6.37 per hour. If he wants to hire 12 workers, how many hours can each put in on Paul's project? How many workers should he hire if he wants each one to put in 850 hours on the project?

10. A glass fiber-optic extrusion machine produces 1.5 meters of fiber per minute. How many complete sections precisely 0.8765 cm long can be cut from a one day's (8 hours) production of the fiber? (1 meter = 100 cm).

Operations With Fractions and Decimals

Learning the Concept

Sometimes you have to find both fractions and decimals in the same problem. You can use what you have learned so far to master this section.

— Adding and Subtracting with Fractions and Decimals —

You can solve such problems with both fractions and decimals by changing all the fractions to decimals *or* by changing all the decimals to fractions. Most of the time you will want to change fractions to decimals because calculators work more often with decimals.

For example, suppose you are asked to add $\frac{2}{3}$ and 0.485. To solve this problem *either* change $\frac{2}{3}$ to its decimal equivalent *or* change 0.485 to its fraction equivalent. If you have memorized the decimal equivalent of certain common fractions, the choice is simple.

In case you haven't, here is a list that will come in handy. (Note that most repeating decimals in this list have been rounded off to two or three decimal places.)

$\frac{1}{2} = 0.5$	$\frac{3}{5} = 0.6$	$\frac{4}{7} = 0.571$
$\frac{1}{3} = 0.33$	$\frac{4}{5} = 0.8$	$\frac{5}{7} = 0.714$
$\frac{2}{3} = 0.67$	$\frac{1}{6} = 0.167$	$\frac{6}{7} = 0.857$
$\frac{1}{4} = 0.25$	$\frac{5}{6} = 0.833$	$\frac{1}{8} = 0.125$
$\frac{3}{4} = 0.75$	$\frac{1}{7} = 0.143$	$\frac{3}{8} = 0.375$
$\frac{1}{5} = 0.2$	$\frac{2}{7} = 0.286$	$\frac{5}{8} = 0.625$
$\frac{2}{5} = 0.4$	$\frac{3}{7} = 0.428$	$\frac{7}{8} = 0.875$

You may not have this chart with you when you need it. Or you may need to find the decimal equivalent of a fraction that is not on the chart. You can always use division to find the decimal equivalent of a fraction. Remember that the fraction line means divided by. So, for example, the fraction $\frac{11}{15}$ means "11 divided by 15." To find the decimal equivalent of $\frac{11}{15}$, just divide 11 by 15. The easiest way to do that is with a calculator, which shows that 11 divided by 15 is equal to 0.733.

— Multiplying and Dividing with Fractions and Decimals —

The simplest way to solve problems with fractions and decimals is to change all fractions to their decimal equivalents. Then you can use a calculator to complete the calculation.

For example, to find the product of $\frac{3}{4}$ times 0.865, the first step is to convert $\frac{3}{4}$ to its decimal equivalent: 0.75. Then you can multiply 0.75 times 0.865 to find the answer of 0.64875.

Another way to solve such problems is to write the decimal part of the problem as a fraction with a denominator of 1. For example, you can set up the problem as follows:

$$\frac{3}{4} \times \frac{0.865}{1}$$

Then, multiply numerator times numerator (3×0.865) and denominator times denominator (4×1) as you would with any fraction.

$$\frac{3}{4} \cdot \frac{0.865}{1} = \frac{3 \times 0.865}{4 \times 1} = \frac{2.595}{4}$$

Divide the numerator (2.595) by the denominator (4) to get the same answer as before, 0.64875.

Handle division problems in a similar way. For example, suppose you are asked to divide $\frac{5}{6}$ by 0.25. The easiest approach is to convert the fraction to a decimal and use a calculator to find the answer. With this method, write the common fraction $\frac{5}{6}$ as its decimal equivalent, 0.833. Then use a calculator to divide 0.833 by 0.25. The answer you get is 3.33.

You can solve this problem another way. Set it up as a division problem and give the decimal a denominator of 1.

$$\frac{5}{6} \div \frac{0.25}{1}$$

Then, remember that the rule for dividing fractions is to invert the divisor and multiply.

$$\frac{5}{6} \times \frac{1}{0.25} = \frac{5 \times 1}{6 \times 0.25} = \frac{5}{1.5} = \frac{1}{0.3}$$

Now you can use the method explained earlier in this chapter to divide 1 by 0.3.

$$
\begin{array}{r}
3.33 \\
0.30.\overline{)1.00.0} \\
\underline{90} \\
10\ 0 \\
\underline{9\ 0} \\
1\ 0\ 0 \\
\underline{9\ 0}
\end{array}
$$

— Solved Examples —

EXAMPLE: Use a calculator to find $\frac{3}{7}$ of 0.8953.

SOLUTION: In problems like this, the word *of* always means "multiplied by." To find $\frac{3}{7}$ of 0.8953, you must multiply $\frac{3}{7}$ by 0.8953. In the chart above, the decimal equivalent of $\frac{3}{7}$ is 0.428. Multiply 0.428 by 0.8953.

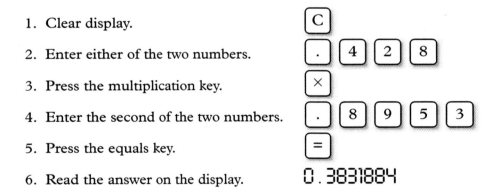

1. Clear display.   C

2. Enter either of the two numbers.   . 4 2 8

3. Press the multiplication key.   ×

4. Enter the second of the two numbers.   . 8 9 5 3

5. Press the equals key.   =

6. Read the answer on the display.   0.3831884

Use a calculator to solve this problem by another method. Think of the problem as follows:

$$\frac{3}{7} \text{ of } 0.8953 = \frac{3}{7} \times \frac{0.8953}{1} = \frac{3 \times 0.8953}{7}$$

1. Clear display.

2. Enter the first number in the numerator.

3. Press the multiplication key.

4. Enter the second number in the numerator.

5. Press the equals key.

6. Press the division key.

7. Enter the divisor.

8. Press the equals key.

9. Read the answer on the display.

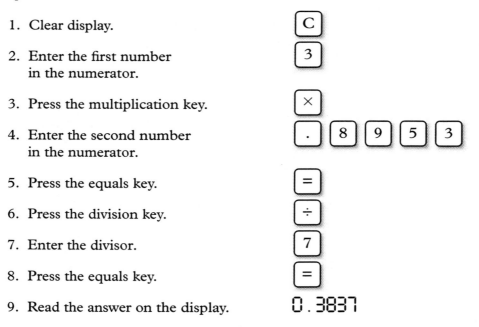

0.3837

Practice Problems

1. Perform each of the indicated operations. Round answers to the nearest thousandth.

   a. $\frac{4}{5} \times 0.75$ _____

   b. $\frac{2}{9} \times 0.343$ _____

   c. $\frac{2}{3} \times 8.69$ _____

   d. $\frac{1}{5} \div 0.25$ _____

   e. $\frac{2}{3} \div 0.875$ _____

   f. $4\frac{1}{2} \div 1.34$ _____

2. Amy is entitled to $\frac{2}{7}$ of the profits of the office supply company she co-owns. If this year's profits are $10,058.32, what is her share of the profits?

   _____

3. The wholesale price of washers from Helmut's hardware store is $1.31 per pound. What is the cost of $10\frac{3}{4}$ pounds of washers?

   _____

4. What is the weight of $3\frac{1}{4}$ boxes of nails if one box weighs 1.275 kilograms? Round your answer to the nearest hundredth.

   _____

5. The nine tilers who work for Marjorie can lay 124.5 square yards of tile on a good day. If they work together, how much tile could two members of the team lay, on average? Round your answer to the nearest hundredth.

   _____

6. A roll of wire holds $10\frac{1}{2}$ yards. How many pieces 2.8 feet long can Norm cut from the roll?

   _____

Percents

Learning the Concept

Percent problems generally ask you to do one of two things: *compare* two numbers by finding the percent that one number is of another or *find* a certain percentage of some number.

— Comparing Numbers —

To find the percent that one number is of another, divide by the number that follows the word *of* in the problem. Express your answer as a decimal. Then change the decimal to a percent.

For example, suppose you are asked to find what percent 6 is of 15. Notice that the number 15 follows the word *of*. That means you must divide by 15.

$$
\begin{array}{r}
0.4 \\
15\overline{)6.0} \\
\underline{60} \\
\end{array}
$$

The answer in decimal form is 0.4. To change *any* decimal to a percent, follow this rule: **Move the decimal point two places to the right and add a percent sign.** For this problem:

$$0.4 \quad = \quad 0.40\% \quad = \quad 40\%$$

— Finding Percentage —

To find percentage, change the percent given to a decimal and multiply by that decimal.

For example, what is 37% of 18?

First, change the percent to a decimal. To change *any* percent to a decimal, follow this rule: **Move the decimal point two places to the left and remove the percent sign.** In this problem:

$$37\% = 0.37$$

Remember that the word *of* means "multiplied by." The next step is to multiply 37% (0.37) by 18.

$$
\begin{array}{r}
1\ \ 8 \\
\times\ 0\,.\,3\ \ 7 \\
\hline
1\ \ 2\ \ 6 \\
5\ \ 4\ \ \ \ \\
\hline
6\,.\,6\ \ 6 \\
\end{array}
$$

Many calculators have a percent key (%) that allows you to calculate an answer directly.

— Solved Examples —

EXAMPLE A: What percent is 13 of 45?

SOLUTION: The divisor in this problem is the number that follows the word *of.* So the problem is 13 ÷ 45.

$$
\begin{array}{r}
.\,2\ \ 8\ \ 8 \\
4\ \ 5\, \overline{)\,1\ \ 3\,.\,0\ \ 0\ \ 0} \\
9\ \ \ \,0\ \ \ \ \ \ \ \ \\
\hline
4\ \ \ \ 0\ \ 0\ \ \ \ \\
3\ \ \ \ 6\ \ 0\ \ \ \ \\
\hline
4\ \ 0\ \ 0 \\
3\ \ 6\ \ 0 \\
\hline
\end{array}
$$

EXAMPLE B: Samantha sells curtains on commission. She earns 5.5% commission on each sale. What is her commission on a sale of $248.50? Use a calculator to solve this problem.

SOLUTION: First, rewrite the problem as a multiplication problem: 5.5% of $248.50 = 5.5% × $248.50. Then,

1. Clear display.
2. Enter the *non-percent* number.
3. Press the multiplication key.
4. Enter the percent.
5. Press the percent key.
6. Press the equals key.
7. Read the answer on the display.

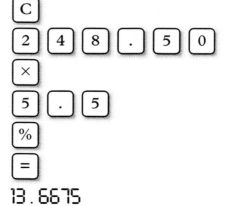

Samantha's commission, to the nearest cent, is $13.67.

Practice Problems

1. In the following problems, find what percent A is of B. Round off all your answers to the nearest tenth.

	a	b	c	d	e
A	6	8	3.7	0.65	$\frac{2}{3}$
B	10	19	4.9	1.89	$\frac{1}{2}$

_____ _____ _____ _____ _____

2. What is C% of D in the following problems?

	a	b	c	d	e
C	25%	10%	42%	3.5%	0.15%
D	60	38	19.5	126	0.3642

_____ _____ _____ _____ _____

3. Manuella sells textbooks on commission. Her commission varies with the amount of the sale. What is her commission on each of the following sales?

Sale	a	b	c	d
Amount of Sale	$5,000.00	$7,500.00	$25,666.75	$10,047.62
Commission	1%	$1\frac{1}{2}$%	2%	$1\frac{3}{4}$%

_____ _____ _____ _____

4. In a shipment of 144 hammers received at Henry's hardware store, 5 were defective. The manufacturer of the hammers promises a 10% deduction in the bill for any shipment in which more than 2% of the items are defective. Is Henry entitled to the deduction?

_____

5. In the dress factory where Ann works, employees earn a bonus of 25% over their regular wages if they complete at least 20% more garments than their target number. For which months in the chart below (if any) did Ann qualify for the bonus?

	March	**April**	**May**	**June**
Target	225	225	250	250
Actual	273	266	296	319

_____   _____   _____   _____

6. Ron is production manager at a plant capable of producing 24,500 bottles per day. Last week the plant produced 20,162; 23,498; and 18,422 bottles on the first three days of the week. At what percent of its total capacity (to the nearest 0.1%) was the plant operating on each of these three days?

_____

7. As food inspector for the city, Xiang checks the composition of ground beef in samples from various stores. What percent fat (to the nearest 0.1%) does he find in each of the samples listed in the table below?

Store	Meyer's	Black Cat	Honest	Sunshine
Total Weight of Sample	2.45 lb	2.39 lb	2.65 lb	2.17 lb
Weight of Fat	0.48 lb	0.39 lb	0.58 lb	0.34 lb

_____   _____   _____   _____

8. Gayle has developed a new low-melting-point alloy consisting of 39.6% copper, 48.8% zinc, and the remainder antimony. What is the weight of each metal in a 58.5-gram sample of the alloy? (Round your answers to the nearest tenth.)

_____

9. A steel bar that originally weighed 15.62 pounds is turned down on a lathe until it weighs 14.48 pounds. What percent of the original bar is waste? (Round your answer to the nearest tenth.)

_____

10. Ted has been asked to increase the dimensions of the floor plan shown in Figure 3.11 to 175% of the original size. What are the dimensions of the new plan?

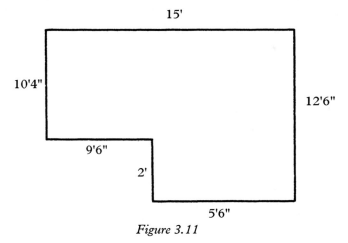

Figure 3.11

CHAPTER FOUR

POWERS, ROOTS, AND GEOMETRIC FIGURES

Roots and Powers

Learning the Concept

Any number multiplied by itself is raised to a power. For example, in the multiplication 4×4, the number 4 appears twice. So 4 is raised to the second **power.** The multiplication 4×4 can also be written another way, 4^2. In this case, the small number ^{2}, the **exponent,** tells how many times the large number 4, the **base,** appears in the multiplication.

$$\text{base} \longrightarrow 4^2 \longleftarrow \text{exponent}$$

The number 6^3 means that the base 6 is raised to the exponent, or power, 3.

$$6^3 = 6 \times 6 \times 6$$

A number raised to the second power is said to be **squared.** You can read the number 10^2 as "10 to the second power" or as "10 squared." A number raised to the third power is said to be **cubed.** You can read the number 5^3 as "5 to the third power" or as "5 cubed." There are no special terms for exponents greater than 3.

Raising a number to a power uses the multiplication skills you have already mastered. For example, suppose you are asked to evaluate 3^4. You now know that 3^4 means $3 \times 3 \times 3 \times 3$. But that is simple multiplication for you: $3 \times 3 \times 3 \times 3 = 81$. So $3^4 = 81$.

Working the other way around is more difficult. We might ask, for example, what number multiplied by itself will give 25. We can ask the same question another way: What is the **square root** of 25? This is the sign for square root: $\sqrt{}$.

We can now ask the question in the following form: $\sqrt{25}$.

Only one number multiplied by itself yields the answer 25. That number is 5, or $\sqrt{25} = 5$.

You might also be asked to find a **cube root.** That means, find the number that multiplied by itself and then again by itself (number $\times$ number $\times$ number) yields a certain value. For example, what is the cube root of 8?

Notice that you put a small 3 in the $\sqrt{}$ part of the operation symbol to write the cube root sign. Cube roots are much harder to guess than square roots. Because $2 \times 2 \times 2 = 8$, the cube root of 8 is 2.

Most calculators have a key for finding square roots and cube roots.

— **Solved Examples** —

EXAMPLE: Use a calculator to find the square root of 47.

SOLUTION: The problem is to find $\sqrt{47}$.

1. Clear display. $\boxed{C}$

2. Enter the number whose square $\boxed{4}$ $\boxed{7}$
   root is to be found.

3. Press the square root key. $\boxed{\sqrt{}}$

4. Read the answer on the display.   6.86

Practice Problems

Use a calculator to perform each of the following operations. If there are more than two decimal places in the answer, round off to the hundredths place.

1. $(11)^2$ _____   6. $(1.2)^3$ _____

2. $(4.2)^2$ _____   7. $\sqrt{81}$ _____

3. $(0.45)^2$ _____   8. $\sqrt{243}$ _____

4. $(12)^3$ _____   9. $\sqrt{0.653}$ _____

5. $(2.1)^3$ _____   10. $\sqrt{0.00592}$ _____

Geometric Figures

Learning the Concept

Roots and powers are common in problems involving geometric figures. Geometric figures, such as squares, rectangles, circles, cubes, spheres, and cones, are constructed with straight and curved lines. A common assignment in many occupations is to calculate the dimensions of a geometric figure.

For example, a farmer may need to find the area of a field to calculate how much fertilizer to buy. Or, a contractor might have to calculate the volume of a swimming pool to meet a client's requirements.

In this section, you will learn about the most common geometric figures.

— Geometric Figures —

Plane figures have only two dimensions, for example, width and length.

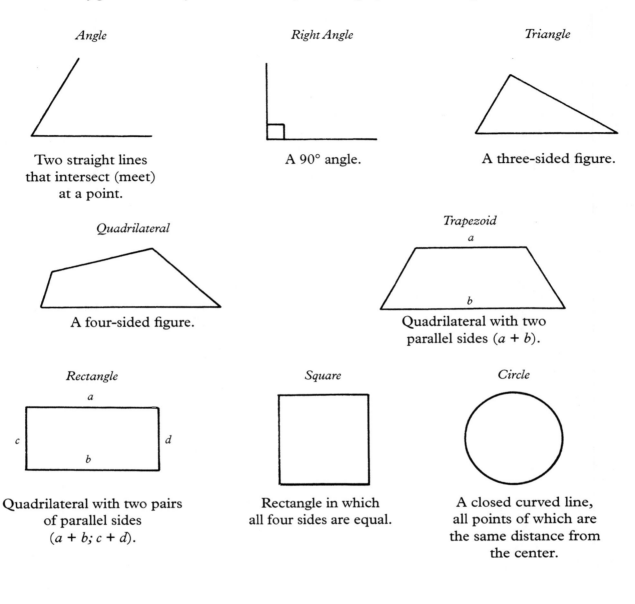

Angle

Two straight lines
that intersect (meet)
at a point.

Right Angle

A 90° angle.

Triangle

A three-sided figure.

Quadrilateral

A four-sided figure.

Trapezoid

Quadrilateral with two
parallel sides ($a + b$).

Rectangle

Quadrilateral with two pairs
of parallel sides
($a + b; c + d$).

Square

Rectangle in which
all four sides are equal.

Circle

A closed curved line,
all points of which are
the same distance from
the center.

Solid figures have three dimensions, for example, length, width, and height.

Prism

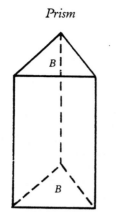

Two triangular bases (*B*).

Cylinder

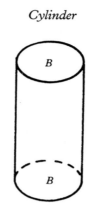

Two circular bases (*B*).

Pyramid

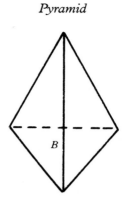

One triangular, rectangular,
or square base (*B*).

Rectangular Solid

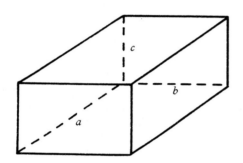

Three rectangles (*a, b, c*)
at right angles to each other.

Cube

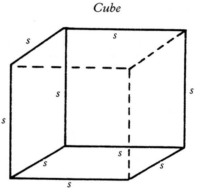

A rectangular box whose sides (*s*)
are the same size.

Cone

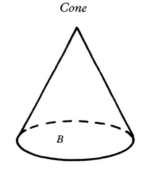

One circular base (*B*).

Sphere

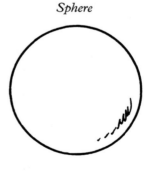

A closed surface, all points on which
are the same distance from its center.

Linear, Angular and Circular Measurement

*Learning
the Concept*

— Perimeters —

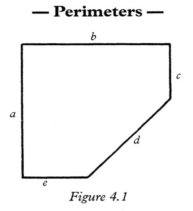

Figure 4.1

The distance around a geometric figure is called its **perimeter.** The perimeter of the corn-field shown in Figure 4.1, for example, is the sum of all five sides of the field. You can express that sum as follows:

$$p = a + b + c + d + e$$

Two widely used perimeter formulas are shown below.

Perimeter of a rectangle:	*Perimeter of a square:*
$p = 2l + 2w$	$p = 4s$
(l = length and w = width)	(s = length of one side)

Expressions such as $2l$, $2w$, and $4s$ mean $2 \times l$, $2 \times w$, and $4 \times s$, respectively. The equations below mean exactly the same thing:

$$p = 4s \qquad p = 4 \times s \qquad p = (4)(s) \qquad p = 4 \cdot s \qquad p = (4) \times (s) \qquad p = (4) \cdot (s)$$

— Angles —

Use the degree symbol [°] to express the size of an angle. A circle contains 360 degrees, or 360°. So 1° is $\frac{1}{360}$ of the way around a circle. Some common angles are shown in Figure 4.2.

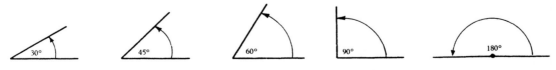

Figure 4.2

Use the minute sign ['] when you divide each degree into minutes for more precise measurements. Use the symbol for a second ["] when you divide each minute of an angle into seconds.

$$1° = 60'   \qquad 1' = 60''$$

— Circumference —

The perimeter of a circle has a special name, **circumference,** usually represented by the letter C. The distance across a circle is called its **diameter,** indicated by the letter D. The distance from any point on the circumference to the center of the circle is called the **radius,** represented by the letter r. The diameter of any circle is equal to twice its radius, or

$$D = 2r$$

A special relationship exists between the circumference of a circle and its diameter, no matter how large or small the circle is. If you divide the circumference by the diameter ($C \div D$), you always get the same number. That number, to the nearest billionth, is 3.141592653. The number is called *pi* and is represented by the Greek letter π. Whenever you see the symbol π, just remind yourself that pi is *a number*—always the same number—and do not think of it as an unknown.

Mathematicians have now calculated the exact value of pi to many thousands of decimal places. For the problems encountered in most occupations, however, you can use the value of 3.14 for pi.

Most calculators have a key for pi, labeled π. When you use this key, instead of entering 3.14, your result will be more precise, with a value carried to many decimal places.

We express the relationship of pi to the circumference C and diameter D of a circle as follows.

$$C = \pi D \quad \text{or} \quad \frac{C}{D} = \pi$$

Because $D = 2r,$

$$C = \pi D$$

$$\text{or } C = \pi \, 2r$$

$$\text{or } C = 2\pi r$$

— Solved Examples —

EXAMPLE A: How much trim does Willard need to go around the perimeter of the floor of a room that is 14'6" long and 8'10" wide?

SOLUTION: In this case, l, the length of the room, is 14'6" and w, the width of the room, is 8'10". Use the formula for the perimeter of a rectangle, $p = 2l + 2w$.

$$p = 2l + 2w$$

$$p = (2 \times 14'6'') + (2 \times 8'10'')$$

To solve this problem, change all the measurements to feet or change them all to inches.

$$14'6" = 14\frac{1}{2}' \text{ or } 174"$$

$$8'10" = 8\frac{10}{12}' = 8\frac{5}{6}' \text{ or } 106"$$

Using the first of these conversions:

$$p = [(2) \times (14\tfrac{1}{2}')] + [(2) \times (8\tfrac{5}{6}')]$$

$$p = [(2) \times \left(\tfrac{29'}{2}\right)] + [(2) \times \left(\tfrac{53'}{6}\right)]$$

$$p = 29' + \tfrac{53}{3}'$$

$$p = 29' + 17\tfrac{2}{3}'$$

$$p = 46\tfrac{2}{3}'$$

EXAMPLE B: Use a calculator to find the circumference of a circle whose radius is 2.3 feet.

SOLUTION: First write the formula for the circumference of a circle: $C = 2\pi r$.

Then substitute the value of the radius given in the problem: $C = (2) \times (\pi) \times (2.3')$.

Then perform the indicated multiplication on the calculator.

1. Clear display. $\boxed{C}$

2. Enter the number 2. $\boxed{2}$

3. Press the multiplication key. $\boxed{\times}$

4. Press the key marked π. $\boxed{\pi}$

5. Press the multiplication key. $\boxed{\times}$

6. Enter the number 2.3. $\boxed{2}\ \boxed{.}\ \boxed{3}$

7. Press the equals key. $\boxed{=}$

8. Read the answer on the display. 14.45136

The circumference of the circle, rounded to the nearest tenth, is 14.5 feet.

Practice Problems

1. What is the perimeter of a triangle with sides that are 3.5", 4.2", and 6.9" long?

_____

2. What is the perimeter of a rectangle with a length of 31.4 cm and a width of 17.9 cm?

_____

3. How much fencing does Olga need to completely enclose her farm, shown in Figure 4.3?

_____

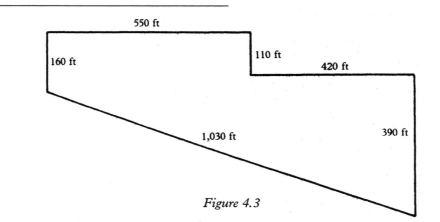

Figure 4.3

4. Amy's job at the print shop is to band together booklets in stacks of 50 each. Each booklet is 11" long, $8\frac{1}{2}$" wide, and $2\frac{3}{4}$" thick (see Figure 4.4). What length of banding material will Amy need if the bands run across the width of the stack? Across the length of the stack?

_____

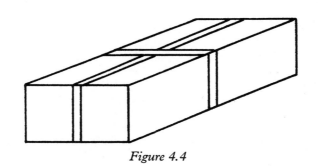

Figure 4.4

5. Velma has to paint a solid red band one quarter of the way around a silo that is 148 feet in diameter. What will the length of the band be? Round your answer to the nearest 0.1 foot.

_____

6. A 1-mile racetrack is laid out in a perfect circle. Use $\pi = 3.14$ to find the track's diameter (to the nearest 0.1 foot).

_____

7. To the nearest 0.01 cm, what is the perimeter of Figure 4.5?

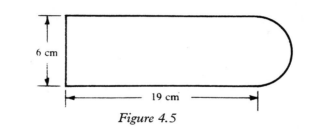

Figure 4.5

8. When Florence wraps a package at her gift shop, she winds the ribbon once around the box in each direction, as shown in Figure 4.6. She allows another 2 feet for the bow. How much ribbon does Florence need to wrap 25 boxes that are 18" long, 14" wide, and $3\frac{1}{2}$" deep?

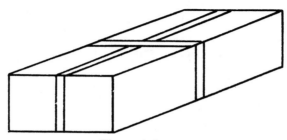

Figure 4.6

Area

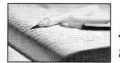

Learning the Concept

There are formulas that allow you to calculate the area of any common geometric figure. A **formula** is a combination of letters and numbers that tells you what numerical operations to perform.

For example, the formula for finding the area of a triangle is:

$$A = \frac{1}{2}bh.$$

To find the area of any triangle, multiply one-half $(\frac{1}{2})$ times the length of its base b times

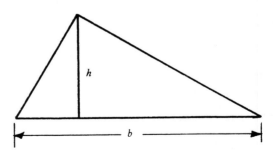

its altitude *h*. The **altitude** of the triangle is the perpendicular (right-angle) distance from any angle of the triangle to the opposite side.

Below are some useful formulas:

Rectangle $A = lw$ l = length
                          w = width

Square $A = s^2$ s = length of a side

Circle $A = \pi r^2$ r = radius of a circle

Trapezoid $A = \frac{h}{2}(b_1 + b_2)$ h = height of trapezoid
                                              b_1 = length of one base
                                              b_2 = length of second base

Below are some useful conversions:

1 square foot = 144 square inches = 12^2 square inches

1 square yard = 9 square feet = 3^2 square feet

— **Solved Examples** —

EXAMPLE A: Find the area of a triangle with a base of 38.5 cm and an altitude of 14.9 cm. Round your answer to two decimal places.

SOLUTION: In solving problems with geometric figures, it may help to make a sketch such as Figure 4.7 and then write the appropriate formula.

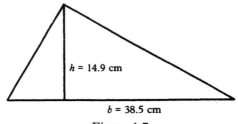

Figure 4.7

$$A = \tfrac{1}{2}bh$$

Substitute the values of *b* (38.5 cm) and *h* (14.9 cm) in the formula.

$$A = (\tfrac{1}{2}) \times (38.5 \text{ cm}) \times (14.9 \text{ cm})$$

Calculate the answer:

$$A = 286.82 \text{ square centimeters (or 286.82 cm}^2)$$

EXAMPLE B: Use a calculator to find the area of a circle whose radius is 5.2". Round your answer to two decimal places.

SOLUTION: To find the area of a circle when the radius is given, use the formula.

$$A = \pi r^2$$

$$A = \pi \times (5.2")^2$$

To solve this problem, perform the multiplications in the order indicated.

1. Clear display.

2. Enter 3.14, or press the π key.

3. Press the multiplication key.

4. Enter the number 5.2.

5. Press the multiplication key.

6. Enter the number 5.2 again.

7. Press the equals key.

8. Read the answer on the display.

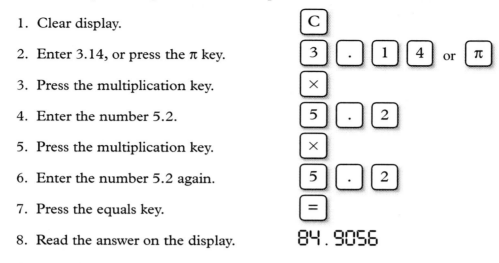

The area of the circle, rounded to the nearest hundredth, is 84.91 inches.

EXAMPLE C: Jarvis wants to find the area of the cotton field shown in Figure 4.8. How can he calculate that area? What is the area of the field?

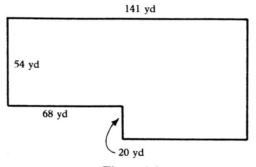

Figure 4.8

SOLUTION: The figure does not look like any of the figures for which you have a formula. But you can sometimes find the area of an unusual figure by breaking it up into smaller pieces whose areas you *can* find. For example, suppose you draw a dotted line in this figure, as shown in Figure 4.9. Then you have two figures, both rectangles, whose areas you know how to calculate.

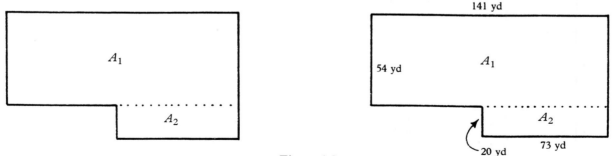

Figure 4.9

For the large rectangle:

$A_1 = lw$

$A_1 = 141 \text{ yd} \times 54 \text{ yd}$

$A_1 = 7,614 \text{ yd}^2$ (square yards)

For the small rectangle:

$A_2 = lw$

$A_2 = 20 \text{ yd} \times 73 \text{ yd}$

$A_2 = 1,460 \text{ yd}^2$

The total area (A_T) of the figure is

$A_T = A_1 + A_2$

$A_T = 7,614 \text{ yd}^2 + 1,460 \text{ yd}^2$

$A_T = 9,074 \text{ yd}^2$

Practice Problems

1. Find the area (to one decimal place) of each of the figures shown below. Use $\pi = 3.14$.

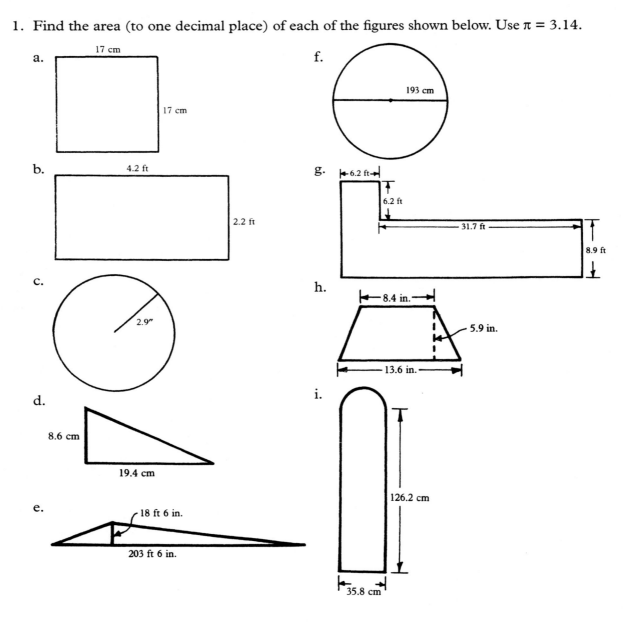

a. 17 cm / 17 cm

b. 4.2 ft / 2.2 ft

c. 2.9″

d. 8.6 cm / 19.4 cm

e. 18 ft 6 in. / 203 ft 6 in.

f. 193 cm

g. 6.2 ft / 6.2 ft / 31.7 ft / 8.9 ft

h. 8.4 in. / 5.9 in. / 13.6 in.

i. 126.2 cm / 35.8 cm

2. Gerard has been hired to paint a fence that is 184 feet long and 6 feet high. What is the total area to be painted? If 1 gallon of paint covers 400 square feet, how many gallons of paint must Gerard buy? At $17.95 per gallon, what will be the total cost of the paint?

    _____

3. Each hat that Donnelly makes in his shop starts out as a circle of felt 28 inches in diameter. What is the area of this initial piece of felt?

    _____

4. What is the area of the brass ring shown in the diagram below?

    _____

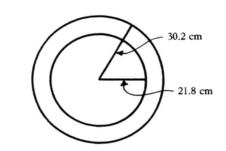

5. Chan has been hired to lay a brick patio in the area shown below. How many 8" × 4" bricks will he need to cover the area? At 45¢ per brick, what is the total cost of these bricks?

    _____

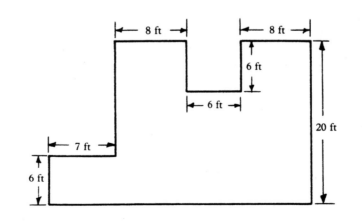

6. What is the area of the cover plate shown below? The diameter of the small holes is $\frac{1}{4}$" and the diameter of the large holes is $1\frac{3}{4}$".

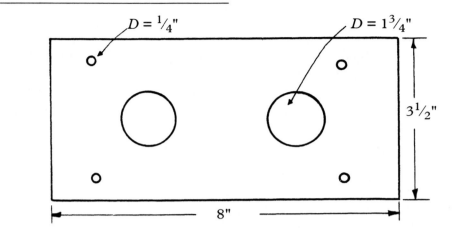

7. Marvin has been hired to paint the water-storage tank shown in Figure 4.10. The tank is 22'6" high and 44'8" in diameter. What is the area of the top of this tank (A in the diagram)? What is the area of the cylindrical part of the tank (K)? What is the total area that Marvin has to paint? Give all answers to the nearest whole number. (*Hint:* Think of the rounded surface, K, as a rectangular sheet wrapped around to form the outside of the tank.)

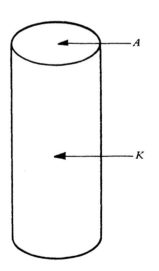

Figure 4.10

8. A new housing development is shown in the plat map (Figure 4.11). What is the area of each of the lots shown on the map?

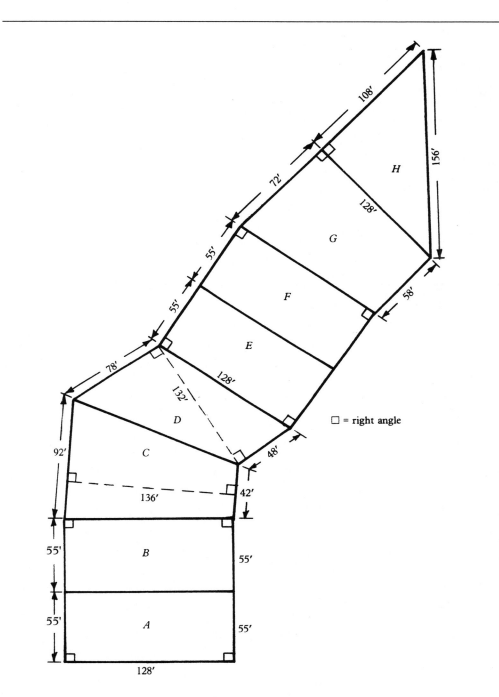

Figure 4.11

Volume

Learning the Concept

The volume of an object is the amount of space inside that object. You can use formulas to calculate the volume of many geometric figures. For example, the formula for the volume of the cone shown in the figure to the right is

$$V = \tfrac{1}{3}\pi r^2 h$$

where *r* stands for the radius of the base and *h* stands for the height of the cone.

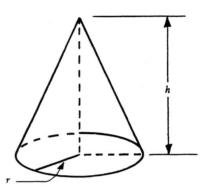

Suppose the cone shown to the right has a base whose radius is 5" and whose height is 11". Calculate the volume of the cone as follows:

$$V = \tfrac{1}{3}\pi r^2 h$$

$$V = \tfrac{1}{3}\pi (5")^2 \times (11")$$

$$V = 287.83 \text{ cubic inches}$$

The label *cubic inches* can also be written as in^3 or as cu in.

Formulas for finding the volume of common geometric figures are given below.

Cube	$V = s^3$	s = length of one side
Rectangular solid	$V = lwh$	l = length w = width h = height (or depth)
Sphere	$V = \tfrac{4}{3}\pi r^3$	r = radius
Cylinder	$V = \pi r^2 h$	r = radius of base h = height of cylinder
Prism	$V = ab \times h$	ab = area of base h = height of prism
Pyramid	$V = -\tfrac{1}{3}(ab) \times h$	ab = area of base h = height of pyramid

Below are some useful conversions:

1 cubic foot = 1,728 cubic inches

1 cubic yard = 27 cubic feet

— Solved Examples —

EXAMPLE A: Find the volume of a sphere whose radius is 3.2".

SOLUTION: Start by writing the formula for the volume of a sphere.

$$V = \frac{4}{3} \pi r^3$$

Substitute the value of r in the formula, and carry out the necessary multiplication.

$$V = \frac{4}{3} \times \pi \times (3.2")^3$$
$$V = 137.19 \text{ in}^3$$

EXAMPLE B: Use a calculator to find the volume of a cylinder whose height is 15.2" and whose base has a radius of 2.5".

SOLUTION: Start by writing the formula for the volume of a cylinder: $V = \pi r^2 h$. Then, substitute the values of r and h in the formula, and use your calculator to carry out the necessary multiplication.

$$V = \pi \times (2.5")^2 \times (15.2")$$

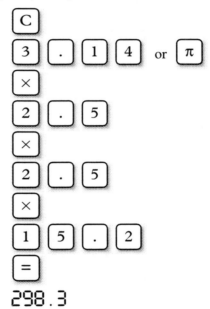

1. Clear display.

2. Enter 3.14, or press the π key.

3. Press the multiplication key.

4. Enter the number 2.5.

5. Press the multiplication key.

6. Enter the number 2.5 again.

7. Press the multiplication key.

8. Enter the number 15.2.

9. Press the equal sign.

10. Read the answer on the display.

Practice Problems

1. Find the volume of each of the figures described below. Round off each answer to no more than two decimal places.

   a. A sphere of radius 28.7 in.

   _____

   b. A cube 52 cm on an edge.

   _____

   c. A rectangular solid that is 22.1" long, 8.6" wide, and 4.7" high.

   _____

   d. A cylinder 1.42 meters high with a circular base with a diameter of 0.92 meters.

   _____

   e. A cone that is 286.7 feet high with a circular base whose diameter is 18 feet.

   _____

2. What volume of paint can Julie store in a can that is 25 inches high with a base 17 inches in diameter? (For conversion, 1 gallon = 231 cubic inches.)

   _____

3. What volume of dirt can Eddie haul in his truck if the truck bed is 10'8" long, 5'10" wide, and 3'2" deep?

   _____

4. The stainless steel pin that Minnie installs in video display units looks like Figure 4.12. What is the total volume of steel used in one of these pins? Round off your answer to one decimal place.

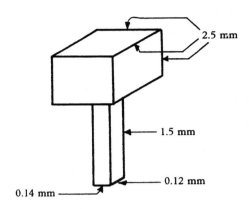

2.5 mm

1.5 mm

0.12 mm

0.14 mm

Figure 4.12

5. The Hard Times Concrete Company is pouring concrete floors for the basements of new houses in the Glossy Willows Housing Development. The number of houses with each basement floor plan is shown below. What is the total amount of concrete, in cubic yards, needed for this job?

Specifications for Basement Floors				
Plan	Number of Houses	Length	Width	Depth
HT-Ax	10	38'6"	20'	6"
HT-Bx	3	32'8"	22'	8"
HT-Cx	16	28'4"	20'	8"

CHAPTER FIVE

MEASURING SYSTEMS AND DEVICES

Measurement

Learning the Concept

How long is the line at the right? _____

Workers in many occupations regularly have to answer a question like that. Carpenters have to find the length of a board. Plumbers need to measure a piece of pipe. Masons have to determine the dimensions of an area to be paved.

Other kinds of measurements are common. A nurse must measure out the right volume of solution to give a patient. A trucker might have to determine a cargo's weight. A cook has to measure the temperature of a batch of candy.

Most people have had at least some experience with measuring length, volume, weight, and temperature. Measuring is part of everyday life. The measurements workers make might require more skill than everyday measurements. For example, a machinist may have to find the length of a metal bar to a hundredth of an inch. In this chapter you will learn some things about measuring that you may not have picked up in your daily life.

— Measurement Error —

For example, you probably don't worry about small errors in measurements you make around the house. If a recipe calls for one cup of chicken stock, the meal will not be spoiled if you use a teaspoon too much or too little. However, in many occupations, workers must make precise, accurate measurements. They must understand how measurement errors occur and what they can do to reduce those errors.

Measurement errors occur for many reasons. The measuring device might be inaccurate. The yardstick could be worn on one edge or manufactured with an imperfection. Machines used to make rulers, yardsticks, scales, and thermometers are not perfect. They can turn out faulty measuring devices.

Humans can make errors when they measure objects. The measuring device may not lie flat on the paper, or a person may not look straight up and down at a line being measured. To demonstrate this point, try using a ruler to measure the line at the top of this page. Make your first measurement looking directly down at the ruler; then try it from various other angles.

Precision and accuracy are especially important in the manufacturing of appliances, tools, and machines. Machines that cut pipe, stamp out washers, or extrude wires, for example, do not always perform perfectly. Machines can be made more accurate, but the cost of improving a machine's accuracy must be weighed against the benefit.

Designers allow a certain margin of error in the *actual* (compared to the *ideal*) manufactured length of pipe, dimensions of a washer, or diameter of a wire, for example. This permissible error is known as **tolerance.** Tolerance is expressed by the ± symbol after a measurement. For example, you might see the length of a metal plate expressed as 35.1 ± 0.1". That means that 35.1" is exactly how long the plate should be, but an error of 0.1" more or 0.1" less in the plate's actual length is acceptable.

Figure 5.1 shows the tolerances allowed in the manufacturing of an aluminum latch front. The table below shows what each tolerance means.

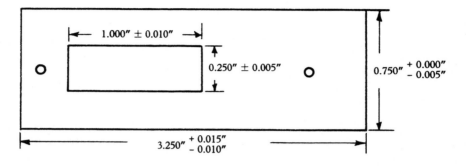

Figure 5.1

Tolerance	Greatest Length Allowed	Least Length Allowed
1.000" ± 0.010"	1.000" + 0.010" = 1.010"	1.000" – 0.010" = 0.990"
0.250" ± 0.005"	0.250" + 0.005" = 0.255"	0.250" – 0.005" = 0.245"
0.750" ± 0.000"	0.750" + 0.000" = 0.750"	0.750" – 0.005" = 0.745"
3.250" ± 0.015"	3.250" + 0.015" = 3.265"	3.250" – 0.010" = 3.240"

The variation from the smallest to the largest allowable dimension is known as the **range of tolerance.** Listed below is the range of tolerance for each of the dimensions in the table:

1. 1.010" – 0.990" = 0.020"

2. 0.255" – 0.245" = 0.010"

3. 0.750" – 0.745" = 0.005"

4. 3.265" – 3.240" = 0.025"

— Measuring Volume —

Some of the devices used for measuring volume are illustrated in Figure 5.2.

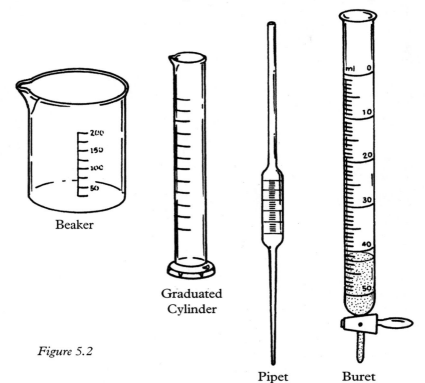

Beaker

Graduated
Cylinder

Pipet   Buret

Figure 5.2

Finding the volume of a liquid involves one special problem. Most liquids have a tendency to creep up along the inside surface of the measuring device, as shown in Figure 5.3a. (Only a few liquids have a tendency to creep downward.)

The curved surface of a liquid in a container is known as the **meniscus.** Measure the volume of the liquid at the bottom of the meniscus, as shown by the dotted line in Figure 5.3b. In this case, you would record 42.7 mL as the volume of the liquid.

Notice that the problem of error in reading volume is similar to the problem in reading length. We know the first two digits of the measurement—42—for certain. But the last digit—.7—is an estimate. Another measurer might write 42.6 mL or 42.8 mL for the same volume. The best way to record the measurement might be 42.7 mL ± 0.1 mL.

Figure 5.3a

Eye level
Bottom of
meniscus

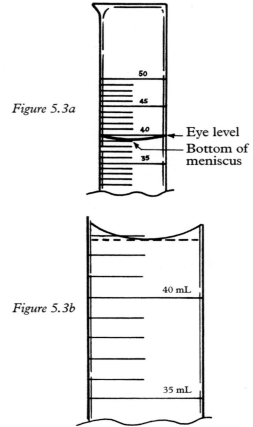

Figure 5.3b

40 mL

35 mL

— Measuring Weight —

Devices for measuring weight are usually called *scales* or *balances*. Some common balances are pictured in Figure 5.4. Today most balances have digital displays.

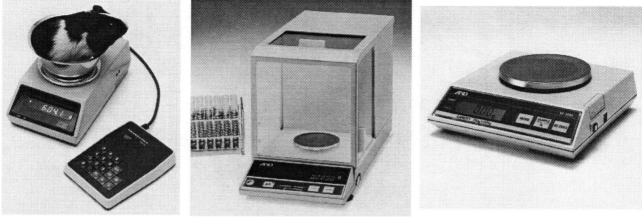

Figure 5.4

The triple-beam balance shown in Figure 5.5 has no digital display. You have to figure out the weight of an object on your own. First, place the object on the pan. Next, move the riders along each of the marked beams until the pointer meets the zero line. Then, read the weight of the object on the marked beams.

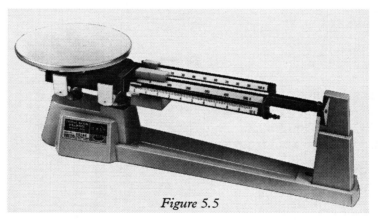

Figure 5.5

Figure 5.6 shows the position of the riders after an object has been weighed. The weight of the object is found by adding the weights shown on each of the four beams.

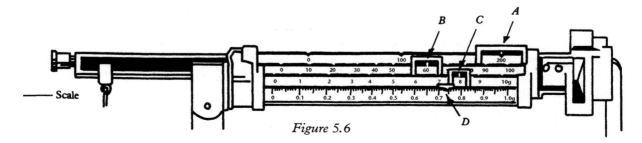

Figure 5.6

Notice that the weight on the beam marked A is 200 grams. The weight on the beam marked B is 60 grams. The weight on the beam marked C is 8 grams. The weight on the bottom beam (D) is about half-way between 0.74 and 0.75. You can show this weight as 0.745 g, with a margin of error ± 0.005 g.

The final weight of the object, then, is

$$200 \text{ g} + 60 \text{ g} + 8 \text{ g} + (0.745 \text{ g} \pm 0.005 \text{ g}) = 268.745 \pm 0.005 \text{ g}$$

Every digit in the answer is known except the last digit, the digit in the thousandths place (the 5). You can indicate the possible error in the answer by including ± 0.005 g.

— Other Measurements —

Workers in some occupations have to use special tools to make measurements. A person who works for the local energy company might have to read gas or electric meters. An electrician must know how to read voltmeters and ammeters. An employee of the water department might have to read a flow meter.

If you know how to read length, volume, and weight measurements, you can learn to make other measurements. It is most important that you know your measuring instruments. Recognize and understand each unit on the device.

Look at the example in Figure 5.7. What volume of water is indicated by this set of home water meters?

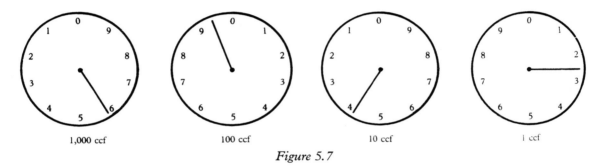

Figure 5.7

Notice that each meter is marked to read a different scale. The meter at the far right reads in hundred cubic feet (ccf). The abbreviation ccf stands for hundred cubic feet. That means that every value on the dial must be multiplied by 100 cubic feet (cf). Notice that the pointer on this dial is between 2 and 3. The pointer is on its way from 2 to 3. The home has used more than 200 cubic feet (2 ccf) but less than 300 cubic feet (3 ccf) of water. (For the purposes of measurement, take the lowest amount you know the home has used, 2 ccf.)

The next dial to the left reads 10 ccf. That means that every number on this dial must be multiplied by 10. The 1 on the dial stands for 1 × 10, or 10 ccf. The 2 stands for 2 × 10, or 20 ccf. The 3 stands for 3 × 10, or 30 ccf, and so on. The pointer on this dial lies between 4 and 5, that is, between 40 (4 × 10) and 50 (5 × 10) ccf of water. The home has used more than 40 ccf of water so far.

The two dials on the left are marked 100 ccf and 1,000 ccf. The 100-ccf label means every value on the dial must be multiplied by 100. The 1,000-ccf label means every value on the dial must be multiplied by 1,000. The readings on these two dials, then, should be recorded as 5,000 ccf (5 × 1,000 ccf) and 900 ccf (9 × 100 ccf).

The total volume of water indicated by these dials is the sum of the four readings, or,

$$5,000 \text{ ccf} + 900 \text{ ccf} + 40 \text{ ccf} + 2 \text{ ccf} = 5,942 \text{ ccf}$$

Notice that the dials are arranged in order of the place value of the digits. Therefore, you can read the volume of water directly from the dials: 5 9 4 2 ccf.

Practice Problems

1. With the most accurate ruler you can find, measure and record the length of each line in the following figures. Include an error term (±xx) that shows the uncertainty of your measurement.

a.

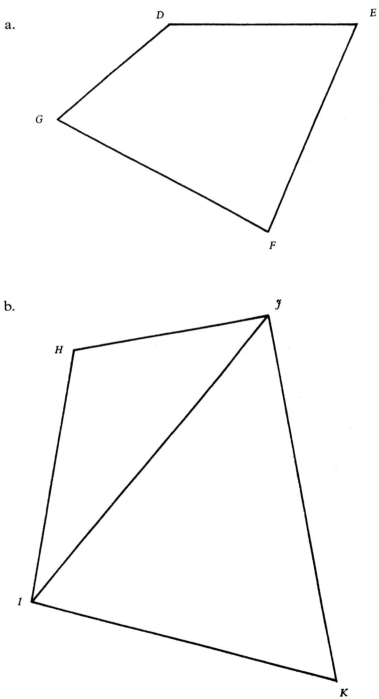

b.

2. Determine the upper limit, the lower limit, and the range of tolerance for each measurement listed below.

   a. $6\frac{1}{4}'' \pm \frac{1}{4}''$

   e. $2.638''\ {}^{+\,0.002''}_{-\,0.000''}$

   b. $8\frac{3}{4}'' \pm \frac{1}{8}''$

   f. $1.041\ cm\ {}^{+\,0.001\ cm}_{-\,0.003\ cm}$

   c. $6.25'' \pm 0.02''$

   g. $2.041'' \pm 0.005''$

   d. $4.75\ cm \pm 0.05\ cm$

   h. $0.793\ mm\ {}^{+\,0.002\ mm}_{-\,0.004\ mm}$

3. What is the volume of the liquid in each of the three graduated cylinders shown in Figure 5.8?

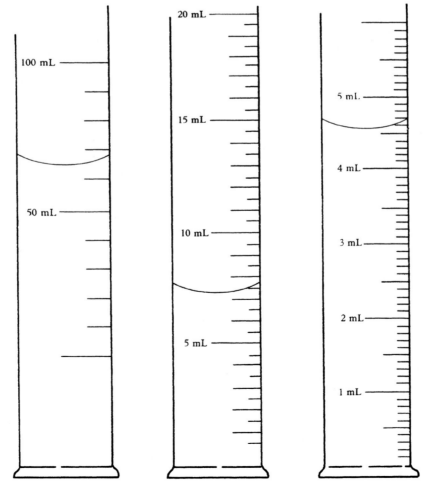

Figure 5.8

4. Read and record the value indicated on each of the water meters shown in Figure 5.9.

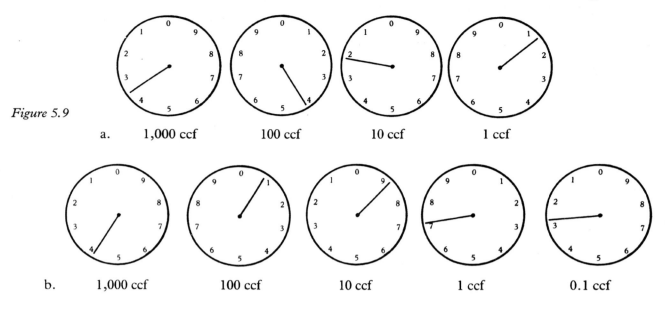

Figure 5.9

   a.   1,000 ccf   100 ccf   10 ccf   1 ccf

   b.   1,000 ccf   100 ccf   10 ccf   1 ccf   0.1 ccf

5. Read and record the value indicated on each of the electrical meters shown in Figure 5.10.

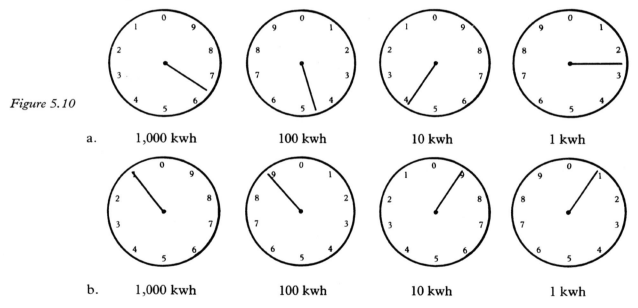

Figure 5.10

   a.   1,000 kwh   100 kwh   10 kwh   1 kwh

   b.   1,000 kwh   100 kwh   10 kwh   1 kwh

Measuring Systems

Learning the Concept

At one time in history, people seldom traveled far from their homes. They did business only with their neighbors. Many towns had their own measuring systems. The world has changed. Travel is easier. Business is conducted across state and national borders. A single worldwide system for measuring length, volume, weight, and temperature would make buying and selling in any part of the world easier.

At present, two measuring systems are widely used. One is the **British system,** with which you are probably familiar. The British system is also called the **customary system.** The British system uses units such as feet and inches to measure length, pounds and ounces to measure weight, pints and quarts to measure volume, and degrees Fahrenheit to measure temperature. The British system is the primary system in only three nations, the United States, Liberia, and Myanmar (formerly, Burma).

The major international measurement system is the **metric system.** The metric system uses units such as centimeters and meters to measure length, grams and kilograms to measure weight, milliliters and liters to measure volume, and degrees Celsius (also called degrees centigrade) to measure temperature. The metric system has been adopted by virtually every country in the world. It is also the system of measurement used by scientists everywhere, including the United States.

Some of the units that make up the British system are listed in the table below. You will recognize most of them. A few may be unfamiliar. The British system grew over many centuries in a haphazard way. Over time, new units were added, and other were lost or forgotten. Some units changed in size.

Some Units in the British Measuring System

Length		Volume	
12 inches (in)	= 1 foot (ft)	4 gills	= 1 pint (pt)
3 ft	= 1 yard (yd)	2 pt	= 1 quart (qt)
$5\frac{1}{2}$ yd	= 1 rod (rd)	4 qt	= 1 gallon (gal)
		231 cubic inches	= 1 gal
320 rd	= 1 mile (mi)	31.5 gal	= 1 barrel (bbl)
1 ell (cloth)	= 45 in	128 cubic feet	= 1 cord (wood)
1 warp (cloth)	= 80 yd	1 noggin	= 1 gill
		1 nebuchadnezzar	= 20 qt (wine)

Weight	
16 ounces (oz)	= 1 pound (lb)
100 lb	= 1 hundredweight (cwt)
20 cwt	= 1 ton
1 lug (cherries)	= 20 lb
1 sack	= 100 lb (flour; U. S. only)

The British system is not really a system. A true measuring system consists of a limited set of related, carefully thought-out units. That description does not fit the British system, as you can see from the table.

In the British system, it is possible to use two different units for measuring volume, depending on whether the material being measured is dry or liquid. Some occupations use a unique measuring system. For example, jewelers and those who work with precious metals employ the *troy system* of weights rather than the *avoirdupois system* shown in the table. In the jewelers' troy system, one pound is equal to 12 ounces. Printers use a special system, also, with units such as a *column inch, em, pica,* and *point.*

Those familiar with British units are accustomed to changing feet to inches, pounds to ounces, and gallons to quarts. The following example introduces a method for making conversions with unfamiliar units.

— Solved Example —

EXAMPLE: Hannah works for a cable television company. In the next week, the company will install 5.8 miles of cable. How many feet of cable will the company install?

SOLUTION: Convert 5.8 miles to feet:

$$5.8 \text{ miles} = ? \text{ feet}$$

You already know—or you could look up—the relationship between feet and miles.

$$5{,}280 \text{ feet} = 1 \text{ mile}$$

This relationship is called a *conversion factor* because it shows how to convert from one unit to another unit. You can write any conversion factor as a fraction whose value is 1. For example, you can write the conversion factor in our example in either of the following ways:

$$\frac{5{,}280 \text{ feet}}{1 \text{ mile}} \qquad \frac{1 \text{ mile}}{5{,}280 \text{ feet}}$$

In both of these fractions, the numerator and denominator are equal to each other. That is, 5,280 feet is equal to 1 mile. Because the numerator and denominator have the same value, the value of the whole fraction is 1. You can multiply any number by 1 without changing the value of the number. That is why you can multiply any number by a conversion factor without changing the value of the number.

You can use a conversion factor to determine how many feet of cable the company will install. Simply multiply the measurement you are given (5.8 miles) by one of the conversion factors. Which one? To start out, we'll tell you. Multiply 5.8 miles by the conversion factor shown below.

$$5.8 \text{ miles} \times \frac{5{,}280 \text{ feet}}{1 \text{ mile}} = \frac{5.8 \text{ miles} \times 5{,}280 \text{ feet}}{1 \text{ mile}}$$

Now go ahead and simplify the fraction. Treat the labels in the fraction just as you treat the numbers. Notice that the mile labels divide out, and the answer will have the label feet.

$$\frac{5.8 \; {}^{1}\cancel{\text{miles}} \times 5{,}280 \text{ feet}}{1 \cancel{\text{mile}}_{1}} = x \text{ feet}$$

Once you multiply and then divide, you get a number to go with the label.

$$\frac{5.8 \ \cancel{\text{miles}}^{1} \times 5,280 \text{ feet}}{1 \ \cancel{\text{mile}}_{1}} = 30,624 \text{ feet}$$

Pick the conversion factor that allows you to divide out and end up with the label you want to see in the answer. You want to know how many feet of cable Hannah's company will install. Use the conversion factor $\frac{5,280 \text{ feet}}{1 \text{ mile}}$ (rather than $\frac{1 \text{ mile}}{5,280 \text{ feet}}$) to end up with the label feet in your answer.

This method gets easier as you practice using it. Conversion factors are the simplest way to solve problems with unfamiliar units. You'll see proof of that in the next section!

Practice Problems

1. Use any method you like to make the following conversions. Round your answers to no more than two decimal places.

    a. 2 ft to inches _____

    b. 40 oz to pounds _____

    c. 2.69 gal to quarts _____

    d. 21.3 bbl to gallons _____

    e. 473 in to yards _____

    f. 0.486 in to feet _____

    g. 14.7 in^3 to pints _____

    h. 3.687 qt to cubic inches _____

2. DJ's catering service has $16\frac{1}{2}$ qt of milk in stock. How many pints is this?

    _____

3. The truck Yee drives contains 40 crates that weigh 385 lb each. The truck itself weighs 2.2 tons. Will Yee be able to drive over a bridge on which the load limit (total weight of vehicle plus contents) is 10 tons?

    _____

4. Dario is packing a shipment of pharmaceuticals. The shipment contains 250 flasks, each holding $6\frac{3}{4}$ gills. What is the total volume, in gallons, of all 250 flasks? (Round your answer to one decimal place.)

    _____

5. How many one-pint canisters can Vincent fill from 2.5 barrels of nails?

    _____

6. Tess plans to make 35 shirts, each of which requires $5\frac{5}{8}$ ft of material. The bolt of cloth holding that material contains 55 yd. Is there enough material on the bolt to make all 35 shirts? How much extra material does she have *or* by how much is she short?

   _____

7. The B-Bar-B ranch measures 1.425 mi on one side, 0.943 mi on a second side, 3.892 mi on a third side, and 5.667 mi on a fourth side. How many full rolls of barbed wire, at 475 ft each, will Esperanza need to buy in order to fence in the ranch completely?

   _____

8. A printer's point is $\frac{1}{72}$ in, and a pica is 12 points. What is the width in inches of a page 48 picas wide? How many points in height is a letter that measures $\frac{1}{3}$ in from top to bottom?

   _____

The Metric System

Learning
the Concept

The metric system is officially recognized around the world. Because of its widespread use in international trade and in science, many U.S. companies now use the metric system as well as the British system.

To use the metric system, keep two ideas in mind.

1. The name of every unit has a logical meaning. You know the size of the unit just by reading its name.

2. The mathematical relationship among units is consistent throughout the system. The metric system is a **decimal system,** that is, a system based on the number 10. Every unit is 10 times, or 10^2 (100) times, or 10^3 (1,000) times, or one-tenth (0.1), or one-hundredth (0.01), or some other multiple of 10 larger or smaller than other units in the system.

Begin your study of the metric system by memorizing the names of the four basic units and learning the system's prefixes. The basic units of measurement in the metric system are as follows (see next page):

length: meter (m)
volume: liter (L)
weight: gram (g)
temperature: degree Celsius (°C)

In the list below, the most common metric prefixes are in boldfaced type. Learn these prefixes by heart and know how to look up the value of the others.

mega- (M)	1,000,000 times
kilo- (k)	1,000 times
hecto- (h)	100 times
deka- (da)	10 times
deci- (d)	0.1 times
centi- (c)	0.01 times
milli- (m)	0.001 times
micro- (μ)	0.000 001 times
nano- (n)	0.000 000 001 times
pico- (p)	0.000 000 000 001 times

Once you know the four basic units and the metric prefixes, you can create units of any size for any kind of measurement. Here are some examples:

A decimeter (dm) = one tenth of a meter, or 0.1 m

A centigram (cg) = one hundredth of a gram, or 0.01 g

A kiloliter (kL) = one thousand liters, or 1,000 L

At first, visualizing the size of the more common metric units may be difficult. You might know what an inch, a pound, and a quart look like but not a meter, a gram, or a liter. The best way to develop familiarity with metric units is to look closely at a meter stick, a one-liter flask, or a set of gram weights. Keep in mind the following approximations.

A meter is about a yard.	A liter is about a quart.
A gram is about $\frac{1}{28}$ oz.	A kilogram is about 2.2 lb.
An inch is about 2.5 cm.	A mile is about 1.6 km.

A **cubic centimeter** (cc or cm^3) is very nearly the same size as a milliliter (mL).

The examples that follow demonstrate how easy the metric system is to use.

— Solved Examples —

EXAMPLE A: Change 2.3 mm to its equivalent in centimeters.

SOLUTION: Solve for x in the equation below.

$$2.3 \text{ mm} = x \text{ cm}$$

You can use a conversion factor to solve for x. You know that

$$1{,}000 \text{ mm} = 1 \text{ m}$$

and

$$100 \text{ cm} = 1 \text{ m}$$

so

$$1 \text{ cm} = 10 \text{ mm}$$

You can express the relationship between millimeters and centimeters in either of two ways:

$$\frac{1 \text{ cm}}{10 \text{ mm}} \quad \text{or} \quad \frac{10 \text{ mm}}{1 \text{ cm}}$$

To solve for x cm, multiply 2.3 mm by the conversion factor that will give you an answer in cm. The question is: Which of the two conversion factors should you write in the box below to make the labels come out right?

$$2.3 \text{ mm} \times \boxed{} = ? \text{ cm}$$

Try writing the conversion factor $\frac{1 \text{ cm}}{10 \text{ mm}}$ in the box and solving for x.

$$2.3 \text{ mm} \times \frac{1 \text{ cm}}{10 \text{ mm}} = \frac{2.3 \ \overset{1}{\cancel{\text{mm}}} \times 1 \text{ cm}}{10 \ \underset{1}{\cancel{\text{mm}}}} = 0.23 \text{ cm}$$

EXAMPLE B: Convert 14.2 milligrams (mg) to kilograms (kg).

SOLUTION: Solve for x in the equation below.

$$14.2 \text{ mg} = x \text{ kg}$$

To solve for x, you need a conversion factor for mg to kg. If you don't know the conversion factor, you do know some conversion factors that will help:

You know that 1 mg = 0.001 g and 1,000 mg = 1 g. And you know that 1 kg = 1,000 g.

So you can work with these conversion factors: $\frac{1{,}000 \text{ mg}}{1 \text{ g}}$ or $\frac{1 \text{ g}}{1{,}000 \text{ mg}}$ and $\frac{1 \text{ kg}}{1{,}000 \text{ g}}$ or $\frac{1{,}000 \text{ g}}{1 \text{ kg}}$.

Decide which conversion factor to write in each of the boxes below in order to make the answer come out in kg.

$$14.2 \text{ mg} \times \boxed{} \times \boxed{} = \text{ kg}$$

Try writing $\frac{1 \text{ g}}{1{,}000 \text{ mg}}$ in the first box.

$$14.2 \text{ mg} \times \frac{1 \text{ g}}{1{,}000 \text{ mg}} \times \boxed{} = \text{ kg}$$

or

$$\frac{14.2 \ \overset{1}{\cancel{\text{mg}}} \times 1 \text{ g}}{1{,}000 \ \underset{1}{\cancel{\text{mg}}}} \times \boxed{} = \text{ kg}$$

Try $\frac{1 \text{ kg}}{1{,}000 \text{ g}}$ in the second box.

$$\frac{14.2 \text{ mg} \times 1 \text{ g}}{1{,}000 \text{ mg}} \times \frac{1 \text{ kg}}{1{,}000 \text{ g}} = \text{ kg}$$

or

$$\frac{14.2 \ \overset{1}{\cancel{\text{mg}}}}{1{,}000 \ \underset{1}{\cancel{\text{mg}}}} \times \frac{1 \ \overset{1}{\cancel{\text{g}}}}{} \times \frac{1 \text{ kg}}{1{,}000 \ \underset{1}{\cancel{\text{g}}}} = \text{ kg}$$

With all labels divided out:

$$\frac{14.2 \times 1 \times 1 \text{ kg}}{1,000 \times 1,000} = 0.000\ 014\ 2 \text{ kg}$$

Practice Problems

1. Convert each of the following measurements to its equivalent in the unit listed.

   a. 5 g to cg _____

   b. 86.3 cg to g _____

   c. 2.35 m to mm _____

   d. 74.58 L to mL _____

   e. 47.9 mL to cc _____

   f. 1,873.4 m to km _____

   g. 58.3 cm to mm _____

   h. 0.427 m to mm _____

2. Faith needs 335.0 mL of solution for each of the 42 patients on her ward. How many liters should she make up for this many patients?

   _____

3. Kwan is installing electrical cable at the convention center. He needs four lengths of cable: 128.5 m, 269.7 m, 194.9 m, and 345.7 m. What is the combined length (in meters) of the cable Kwan needs?

   _____

4. Ferne has received a shipment of electronic parts from a supplier. The shipment contains boxes of many sizes. What is the total weight of the four boxes in the shipment listed below?

   Box 1: 4.38 kg
   Box 2: 875 g
   Box 3: 1.29 kg
   Box 4: 2.33 kg

   _____

5. Dominique is preparing a solution for the laboratory where she works. What will the total volume be if she makes the solution by mixing five chemicals in the following volumes: 350 mL, 1.75 L, 250 mL, 375 mL, and 1.33 L?

   _____

6. Mason pays 92.5¢ for a kilogram of washers. He buys 100 that weigh 20 g each, 250 that weigh 37.5 g each, and 125 that weigh 55.5 g each. What is the total cost of the washers?

    _____

7. Ambrose has been asked to find the total weight of four samples of plastic. The weights of each of those four samples are as follows: 309: 3.58 g, 315: 2.69 g, 323: 356 cg, and 359: 289 cg.

    _____

8. Inez is making a solenoid. One section has 4,275 turns around a core that is 1.45 m in diameter, and another section has 8,325 turns around a core that is 68.72 cm in diameter. What is the total length of wire, in kilometers, that she will need to make this solenoid?

    _____

Measuring Devices

Learning the Concept

Many occupations require specialized measuring instruments. For example, a physician's assistant may use a graduated syringe to give a patient an inoculation (a "shot") of just the right volume. A worker in a steel mill measures the temperature of a blast furnace with a special kind of thermometer that measures thousands of degrees.

Some of the measuring devices you may encounter are shown in the photographs below.

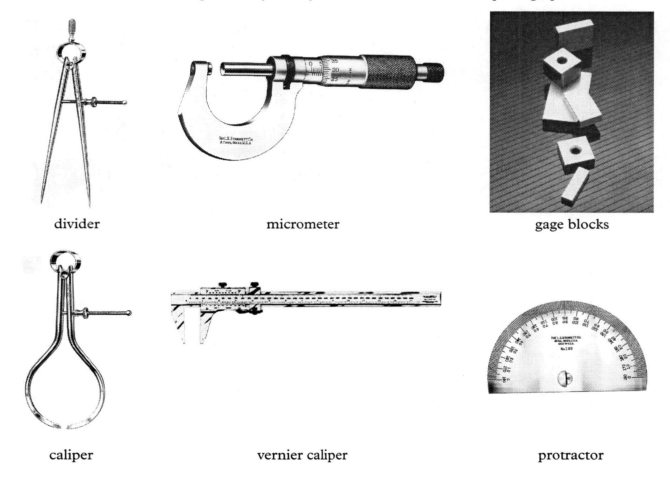

divider   micrometer   gage blocks

caliper   vernier caliper   protractor

A **divider** transfers a measured length from one location to another. In Figure 5.11, the divider has been set at a length of $2\frac{1}{8}$ ". Once the length is set, the divider can be lifted from the ruler and transferred to a board, a sheet of paper, a piece of plastic, a length of pipe, or some other material on which a length of $2\frac{1}{8}$ " needs to be marked off.

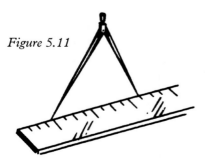

Figure 5.11

Use a **caliper** for distances that are difficult to measure with a standard ruler. Use an inside caliper, shown in Figure 5.12a, to measure the inside dimension of an object. To measure the inside diameter of a pipe, for example, insert the caliper into the pipe and open it fully. Then withdraw the caliper and set it on a ruler, as shown in Figure 5.12b. Read the inside diameter of the pipe on the ruler.

Figure 5.12a   *Figure 5.12b*

The shape of an outside caliper allows it to be used to measure the outside dimensions of an object, as shown in Figures 5.13a and 5.13b. A caliper is accurate to $\frac{1}{64}$ " when the ruler is divided into fractions of an inch, or to $\frac{1}{100}$ " when the ruler is divided into decimal parts of an inch.

Figure 5.13a   *Figure 5.13b*

For more precision, use a **micrometer.** The parts of a metric micrometer are shown in Figure 5.14. The object to be measured is placed between the *anvil* (which does not move) and the *spindle* (which does move). Turn the thimble of the micrometer until the spindle fits snugly against the object. Read the width of the object along the barrel of the micrometer.

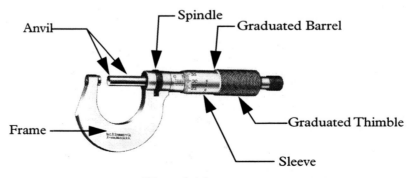

Figure 5.14

Figure 5.15 shows a close-up of a metric micrometer setting.

Figure 5.15

Each upper division on the barrel represents 1.00 mm. The lower divisions mark the upper divisions into 0.5-mm parts. Notice that you can see the marking 5 on the barrel. The thimble has just turned past the next lower division. So the reading is 5.5 mm plus the reading on the thimble.

To complete the reading, look closely at the numbers on the thimble. Each division on the thimble represents a length of 0.01 mm. In this case, the line that marks the number 28 lines up exactly with the long horizontal line on the barrel. To read the setting:

$$
\begin{array}{r}
5.5 \text{ mm} \\
+\ 0.28 \text{ mm} \\
\hline
5.78 \text{ mm}
\end{array}
$$

A **vernier caliper** can also be used to make very precise measurements. The parts of a vernier caliper are shown in Figure 5.16.

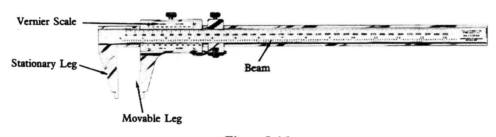

Figure 5.16

Slide the vernier caliper's moveable leg back and forth until it fits precisely in or around an object. You can read the measurement by looking at the scale on the moveable leg, as shown in Figure 5.17.

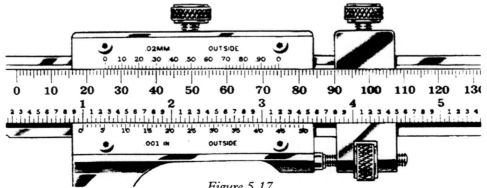

Figure 5.17

Look first at the scale on the beam (the caliper's ruler). You can see part of the scale in Figure 5.17. The full scale reads from 0 to 14 inches along the lower edge and from 0 to 350 mm along the upper edge.

To read the measurement shown in Figure 5.17 in inches, note the 0 mark on the sliding lower vernier scale. In this case, the 0 matches up perfectly with the number 1 on the lower beam scale. Because these marks line up exactly, you can record the measurement as 1.000 in.

To read the same measurement in millimeters, note the position of the 0 mark on the upper vernier scale. It rests just beyond the 25-mm mark on the upper beam scale. Without a vernier scale, it would be difficult to read this measurement more accurately than 25 mm.

The vernier scale allows the measurement in millimeters to two decimal places. To make this measurement, look carefully for the line on the vernier scale that lines up exactly with any line on the beam scale. In this example, the vernier line marked 40 lines up exactly with the line marked 45 on the beam scale. Record the number on the vernier scale. The final measurement in Figure 5.17 is 25 mm + 0.40 mm or 25.40 mm.

Both measurements, in inches and in millimeters, are comparable to each other: 1.000 in = 25.40 mm.

Gage blocks are among the most accurate of common measuring devices. Gage blocks are manufactured to stack one on top of the other to produce a thickness that is accurate within millionths of an inch.

A **protractor** measures the size of angles. The simple protractor, familiar to most math students, is shown in Figure 5.18. The scale on the protractor reads in degrees (°), from 0° to 180°. Each line on the protractor represents one degree (1°). You can read a protractor from left to right or from right to left.

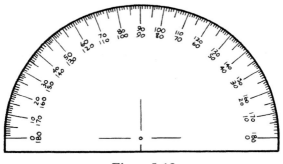

Figure 5.18

Place the protractor so that the small circle at the center of the lower edge meets the *vertex* of the angle. Line up one side of the angle with the 0° mark on the protractor. Then find the line on the protractor that corresponds to the second side of the angle. Figure 5.19 shows an 83° angle.

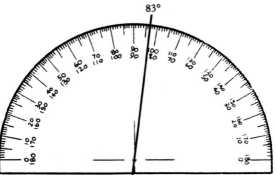

Figure 5.19

Practice Problems

1. Read and record the measurements indicated by each of the metric micrometer settings pictured below.

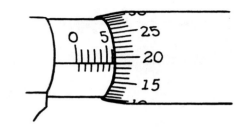

a. _____

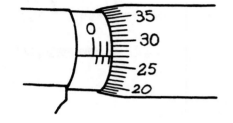

b. _____

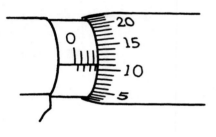

c. _____

d. _____

2. Read and record the measurement indicated by each of the vernier caliper settings shown below.

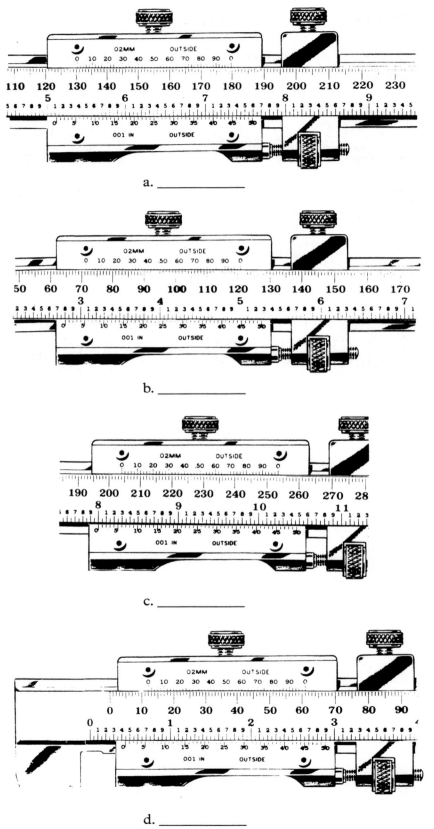

a. _____

b. _____

c. _____

d. _____

3. Use a protractor to measure each of the angles in the figures below. Record your answers for angles *a* through *h*.

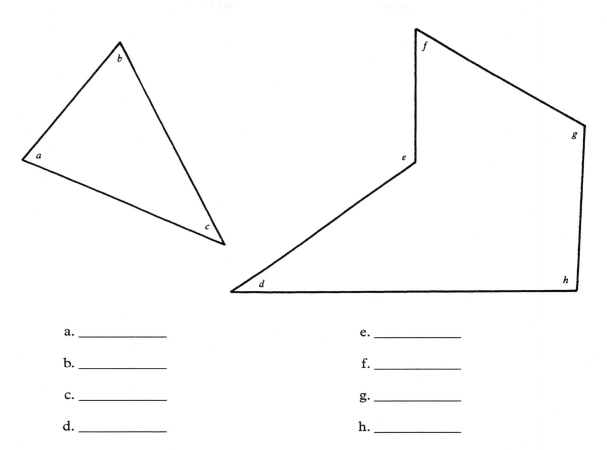

a. _____   e. _____

b. _____   f. _____

c. _____   g. _____

d. _____   h. _____

MATHEMATICAL FORMULAS; RATIOS AND PROPORTIONS

Mathematical Formulas

Learning the Concept

A **mathematical formula** is any combination of letters and numbers joined by an equal sign. You have already used some mathematical formulas in the chapter on geometric figures. For example, the formula for finding the circumference of a circle is

$$C = \pi D$$

A formula is a kind of **equation.** An equation consists of two sets of numbers and/or letters joined by an equal sign. The left side of the equation above is the letter C. The right side is the expression πD. The equal sign (=) says that the two sides of the equation are equal to each other. That is, the equation says that the circumference of a circle (C) is exactly equal to the product of pi (π) and the diameter of the circle (D).

Equations and formulas look alike. Just by looking, you can't tell whether $y = mx + b$ is an equation or a formula. You may encounter the term *formula* when figuring the interest owed on borrowed money ($i = prt$) or finding the volume of a given sample of gas ($pv = nRT$).

The letters used in a formula stand for some real physical things. Consider the formula for the perimeter of a rectangle, $p = 2l + 2w$. In this formula, p stands for the perimeter of the rectangle, l for its length, and w for its width. A formula is a way to convert a sentence into a mathematical statement. The formula $p = 2l + 2w$ is just a mathematical way to write the sentence: "The perimeter of a rectangle is equal to twice its length added to twice its width."

Formulas are easy to work with if you remember one simple rule: You can do the same thing to *both sides* of an equation without changing its meaning or value. Think of an equation as a balance with weights on the left side and an object on the right side. Add the same amount to both sides, and the scale is still balanced. Take away (subtract) the same amount from both sides, and the scale is still balanced. Multiply or divide both sides by the same number, and the scale remains balanced. (The only exception is that you cannot divide by 0.)

We can prove this point with a very simple equation. You know that:

$$8 = 5 + 3$$

Now try adding the same number (any number) to both sides of the equation. For example, add the number 4 to both sides of the equation.

$$8 + 4 \overset{?}{=} 5 + 3 + 4$$

(The ? over the equal sign means we are testing to see if the statement of equality is true or not.)

On the left of this equation is 8 + 4 = 12. On the right is 5 + 3 + 4 = 12. So we still have an equal relationship after adding the same number to both sides of the equation.

The key words are **same number** and **both sides.**

Try to prove the next part of the rule by subtracting some number (the same number) from both sides of the equation. For example, subtract 6 from both sides of the equation. What result do you get?

To show how multiplication affects the equation, suppose we multiply both sides of the equation by 7.

$$8 \times 7 \overset{?}{=} (5 + 3) \times 7$$

Then, on the left, 8 × 7 = 56. On the right, multiply 5 × 7 and 3 × 7 and add the answers.

$$5 \times 7 = 35 \qquad 3 \times 7 = 21 \qquad 35 + 21 = 56$$

You can see that performing the same operation on both sides of the equation maintains the equality. See if you can show that dividing both sides of an equation by the same number also maintains the equality.

— Solving Formula Problems —

Formulas are general statements. They apply to all possible examples. For example, the formula $C = \pi D$ means that the circumference of *any* circle is equal to pi times the diameter. The circumference of *every* circle is equal to pi times the diameter. You can always use the formula $C = \pi D$, in any occupation. It makes no difference if you are a machinist, a plumber, or an architect's assistant.

Workers use formulas when they have to find out about specific situations. Suppose your work as a gardener requires you to lay out a circular patio. You want to know how much fence you will need to go around the patio. You can measure the diameter of the patio. Assume that you find the diameter of the patio is 35 feet across.

Now you can use the formula for finding the circumference of a circle. That formula applies to your circular patio, just as it does to any other circle in the world. That is, you know that for all circles:

$$C = \pi D$$

You know that for your circular patio, $D = 35'$. So, you can substitute the value of D (35') in the formula:

$$C = \pi \times 35'$$

Calculate the value of C. Use 3.14 for the value of π, or use a calculator to determine the answer. Either way, you find that

$$C = 109.9' \text{ (rounded to the nearest whole unit, } 110')$$

Suppose that your patio fencing problem is whether 65 feet of fencing is enough to enclose a circular patio 20 feet in diameter.

You can still use the circumference formula. This time you know the circumference ($C = 65$ feet), not the diameter. That's not a problem! You can substitute the value you know in the formula:

$$C = \pi D$$

$$C = 65'$$

$$65' = \pi D$$

Solve this equation for D.

You have just learned how to solve a problem very much like this. Recall that you can always add, subtract, multiply, or divide without changing the equality, as long as you do the same to both sides of the equation.

Your goal is to get the unknown quantity (D) by itself on one side of the equation. In this equation, D is not alone. D is multiplied by π. In order to get D by itself, you have to *un*do the multiplication. You have to do the *opposite* of multiplication. The opposite of multiplication is division. To get D by itself in the equation, look at the number (π) by which D is multiplied. Divide both sides of the equation by that number: $65' \div \pi = D / \pi$

$$\frac{65'}{\pi} = \frac{\pi \times D}{\pi}$$

In this case, see what happens when you divide both sides of the equation by π.

$$\frac{65'}{\pi} = \frac{{}^1\!\!\!\!\not\pi \times D}{{}^1\!\!\not\pi}$$

Now you have an equation you can solve.

$$\frac{65'}{\pi} = D$$

Do the calculation $65' \div \pi$ to get the answer.

$$D = 20.7'$$

Look at another example. The formula for the perimeter of a triangle is

$$p = a + b + c$$

where a, b, and c are the lengths of the three sides of the triangle.

Suppose you want to find the length of the third side (c) of a triangle whose perimeter (p) is 29.5" and whose other two sides are 11.4" (a) and 8.9" (b). You already know that

$$p = 29.5" \qquad a = 11.4" \qquad b = 8.9"$$

Substitute these known values into the formula,

$$p = a + b + c$$

or

$$29.5" = 11.4" + 8.9" + c$$

Add 11.4" + 8.9".

$$29.5" = 20.3" + c$$

Now the only unknown quantity is c. To get c by itself, perform the operation that is the opposite of addition, namely, subtraction, on both sides of the equation.

$$29.5" - 20.3" = 20.3" - 20.3" + c$$

or

$$9.2" = c$$

The length of the third side (c) is 9.2".

— Solved Examples —

You can use a calculator to solve formula problems. Start by solving the formula for your unknown. Look at the example below.

EXAMPLE A: Find the width w of a rectangular solid whose volume V is 396 cubic inches, whose length l is 11 inches, and whose height h is 4 inches.

SOLUTION: Write the formula for finding the volume of a rectangular solid.

$$V = lwh.$$

Before you substitute known values, set up the formula to solve for your unknown quantity, w.

$$w = \text{something}$$

Notice that in the original formula, w is multiplied by l and h. To get w by itself, *un*do the multiplication: Divide both sides of the equation by l and h.

$$\frac{V}{lh} = \frac{lwh}{lh}$$

Notice that lh divides out on one side of the equation:

$$\frac{V}{lh} = \frac{\cancel{l}wh\cancel{^1}}{\cancel{lh}\cancel{^1}}$$

$$\frac{V}{lh} = w$$

Now substitute your known values.

$$V = 396 \text{ in}^3 \qquad l = 11 \text{ in} \qquad h = 4 \text{ in}$$

$$w = \frac{396 \text{ in}^3}{11 \text{ in} \times 4 \text{ in}}$$

or

$$w = \frac{396 \text{ in}^3}{44 \text{ in}^2}$$

and

$$w = 9 \text{ in}$$

You can always solve the formula before you substitute in known values—whether or not you use a calculator. Solving the formula first saves time, especially when you use the same formula again and again.

EXAMPLE B: Find the width w of a rectangle whose perimeter p is 148 in and whose length l is 43 in.

SOLUTION: Write the formula for finding the perimeter of a rectangle.

$$p = 2l + 2w$$

In this example, the unknown is the width w. Your goal is to get w by itself on one side of the equation. Notice that in this case two things have been done to the w: The w has been multiplied by 2 and added to $2l$.

The rule is to *un*do addition and subtraction first. In this example, subtract $2l$ from both sides of the equation.

$$p - 2l = 2l - 2l + 2w$$

or
$$p - 2l = 2w$$

Now *un*do the multiplication by dividing both sides of the equation by 2.

$$\frac{p - 2l}{2} = \frac{2w}{2}$$

$$\frac{p - 2l}{2} = \frac{\overset{1}{\cancel{2}}w}{\underset{1}{\cancel{2}}}$$

$$\frac{p - 2l}{2} = w$$

Now you can substitute known values and solve for w.

$$p = 148" \qquad l = 43"$$

$$w = \frac{148" - (2 \times 43")}{2}$$

$$w = \frac{148" - 86"}{2}$$

$$w = \frac{62"}{2}$$

$$w = 31"$$

Of course, you can also solve any formula problem by substituting known values and then solving the equation directly.

Practice Problems

1. Solve each of the following formulas for the boldfaced letter.

   a. $V = i\mathbf{r}$ _____

   b. $p = i^2\mathbf{r}$ _____

   c. $c = \mathbf{f}\lambda$ _____

   d. $v = \mathbf{v_0} + at$ _____

   e. $C = \dfrac{\pi \mathbf{D} r}{12}$ _____

   f. $\mathbf{v_0} = \dfrac{2\pi A}{T}$ _____

2. Jason's farm covers a rectangular plot of 450 acres. One side of the farm is 6,340 feet long. How long (to the nearest foot) is the second side? (1 acre = 43,560 square feet.)

   _____

3. The silo owned by the Lone Star Co-op holds 1.4 million cubic feet. If the silo is 220 feet tall, what is the diameter of its base?

   _____

4. Li's longest ladder is 45'6" (*c*) long. If he places the ladder 8'6" (*b*) from the side of a house, what is the highest point on the house the ladder can reach (*a*)? (*Hint:* Figure 6.1 shows how the ladder will lean against the house. Use the Pythagorean Theorem formula $a^2 + b^2 = c^2$.)

   _____

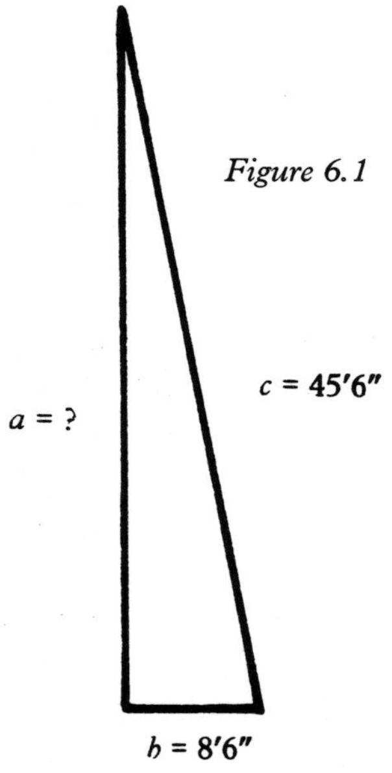

Figure 6.1

$c = 45'6''$

$a = ?$

$b = 8'6''$

5. When most metals are heated, they expand. The amount by which they expand (Δl) depends on their original length (*l*), the change in temperature (ΔT), and a characteristic property of the metal itself (α). The formula that relates these quantities is:

$$\Delta l = l\alpha\Delta T$$

Winston wants to determine what change in temperature will cause an aluminum beam 200 m long to expand by 5 cm. The value of α for aluminum is 0.000026. Your answer will be in degrees Celsius (°C).

   _____

6. At his shop, Warren uses a hydraulic jack made of two pistons connected by a fluid. In the formula below, F_1 and F_2 represent the forces on the two pistons. A_1 and A_2 stand for the areas of the two pistons.

$$\frac{F_1}{F_2} = \frac{A_1}{A_2}$$

What force is exerted on a piston with a 250-square-inch surface area when a force of 100 pounds is applied to a piston with a surface area of 12.5 square inches?

_____

7. Ned must occasionally make power calculations for the circuits in the plant where he works. He uses the following formula to make his calculations.

$$P = i^2 r$$

P is the power in watts, i is the current in amps, and r is the resistance in ohms. How much current i flows through a circuit with a resistance r of 12.52 ohms and a power output p of 15,500 watts?

_____

8. Franny uses a cutting tool that is 10" in diameter d. It has a maximum cutting speed C of 48.5 feet per minute. Franny uses the formula below to calculate how fast the wheel revolves R at maximum speed:

$$C = \frac{\pi dR}{12}$$

C is the cutting speed, in feet per minute; d is the tool's diameter, in inches; and R is the speed of the wheel, in revolutions per minute. How fast does the wheel revolve at maximum speed?

_____

Ratios and Proportions

Learning the Concept

A **ratio** is a way of comparing two quantities by means of division. The expression $\frac{\$4,000}{\$2,000}$ is a ratio because it compares one value with another by means of division.

Suppose that Meredith wants to compare the volume of water that flows from a pipe with the diameter of the pipe. Let V stand for the volume of water. Let d stand for the diameter of the pipe. There are three ways to express a ratio:

$$\frac{V}{D} \quad \text{or} \quad V : d \quad \text{or} \quad V \div d$$

Simply stating a ratio in one of these forms may be sufficient. Or you may be expected to express the ratio in simpler form. For example, suppose you have been asked to find the compression ratio in a gasoline engine. A compression ratio compares the volume of a cylinder when the piston is at the bottom of the cylinder to the volume when the piston is at the top of the cylinder. Suppose you know that the volume of the cylinder with the piston at the bottom is 28 cc and that the volume of the cylinder with the piston at the top is 7 cc. One way to express the compression ratio is 28 cc : 7 cc, or

$$\frac{28 \text{ cc}}{7 \text{ cc}}$$

But the general form for compression ratios is $a : 1$.

To change your compression ratio (28 cc : 7 cc) to the $a : 1$ form, divide both parts of the fraction by the same number.

$$28 \text{ cc} \div 7 \text{ cc} = 4$$

and

$$7 \text{ cc} \div 7 \text{ cc} = 1$$

Your compression ratio is 4 : 1.

It is common to express a ratio in lowest terms. Suppose you are asked to find the ratio of a 42-in line to a 70-in line. It is perfectly acceptable to express the ratio as 42" : 70". But, with a little thought, you can see that both terms of the ratio can be divided by the same number, 14.

$$42" \div 14 = 3$$

and

$$70" \div 14 = 5$$

Reduced to lowest terms, the ratio is 3 : 5.

The most common use of ratios is in **proportions.** A proportion is a set of equal ratios. The expression below is a proportion because it says that two ratios (a/b and c/d) are equal to each other.

$$a/b \ = \ c/d$$

Another way of writing the same proportion is $a : b = c : d$

In any proportion, the first and last terms (a and d in this example) are called the **extremes.** The middle terms (b and c in this example) are the **means.** A simple rule relates the terms of a proportion: **The product of the extremes equals the product of the means.** In the proportion shown above:

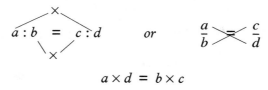

$$a \times d = b \times c$$

When ratios are expressed as fractions, the pairs of numbers are multiplied across the equal sign. So the process of multiplying the extremes and means is sometimes called *cross-multiplication.*

— Solved Examples —

EXAMPLE A: After many years working as a caterer, Bert has learned that he needs about 16 shrimp to feed every 5 people at a party. He would like to know how many shrimp he needs to feed a party of 28 people.

SOLUTION: The key here is the *known ratio.* Bert knows that 16 shrimp feed 5 people. That fact can be expressed as a ratio:

$$16 \text{ shrimp} : 5 \text{ people} \qquad \text{or} \qquad \frac{16 \text{ shrimp}}{5 \text{ people}}$$

Bert makes the assumption that the 28 people at his next party will eat shrimp at the same rate as people have in his past experience. He assumes that 16 shrimp will feed 5 people. He is not expecting to encounter 28 shrimp pigs who will eat a dozen shrimp each or 28 people who hate shrimp and won't eat any at all.

Bert assumes that the ratio of shrimp to people at his party of 28 will be the same as it has been in the past. What is that ratio?

The letter x is often used to stand for some number whose value is unknown. Let x stand for the number of shrimp Bert needs for the party. The ratio of shrimp to people at the party becomes x shrimp : 28 people.

Bert assumes that the ratio of shrimp to people remains the same.

$$16 \text{ shrimp} : 5 \text{ people} = x \text{ shrimp} : 28 \text{ people}$$

or

$$\frac{16 \text{ shrimp}}{5 \text{ people}} = \frac{x \text{ shrimp}}{28 \text{ people}}$$

Include labels in every proportion. Labels allow you to compare terms in the correct order.

To solve for x, use the law of proportions: In a proportion, the product of the means equals the product of the extremes. Cross-multiply.

$$\frac{16 \text{ shrimp}}{5 \text{ people}} = \frac{x \text{ shrimp}}{28 \text{ people}}$$

$$(16 \text{ shrimp}) \times (28 \text{ people}) = (x \text{ shrimp}) \times (5 \text{ people})$$

or

$$x = \frac{(16 \text{ shrimp}) \times (28 \text{ people})}{(5 \text{ people})}$$

$$x = 89.6 \text{ shrimp}$$

Bert will need about 90 shrimp to feed the 28 guests at the party.

All proportion problems have the same format. You can solve any proportion ($a/b = c/d$) if you know three of the four terms in the proportion. (If you know fewer than three terms, you can't solve the proportion.) Solving a proportion always involves the same two steps:

1. Cross-multiply.

2. Solve for the unknown by division.

Your answer will always look like one of the four expressions below:

$$a = \frac{b \times c}{d} \quad \text{or} \quad b = \frac{a \times d}{c} \quad \text{or} \quad c = \frac{a \times d}{b} \quad \text{or} \quad d = \frac{b \times c}{a}$$

No other possibilities exist.

Because all proportion problems have the same format, it's easy to use a calculator to solve a proportion. Look at the following example.

EXAMPLE B: Moab knows that spreading 200 pounds of fertilizer on each acre of his fields increases his yield of corn by 65 bushels per acre. If all other factors stay the same, by how much will his yield increase if he uses 350 pounds of fertilizer per acre?

SOLUTION: In this problem, let x stand for the increase in yield per acre with 350 pounds of fertilizer. The known ratio of fertilizer to increase in yield is

200 pounds : 65 bushels

and the unknown ratio is

350 pounds : x bushels

Use this information to write a proportion.

$$\frac{200 \text{ lb}}{65 \text{ bushels}} = \frac{350 \text{ lb}}{x \text{ bushels}}$$

To solve the proportion, cross-multiply.

$$(200 \text{ lb}) \times (x \text{ bushels}) = (350 \text{ lb}) \times (65 \text{ bushels})$$

Then solve for the unknown:

$$x = \frac{(350 \text{ lb}) \times (65 \text{ bushels})}{(200 \text{ lb})}$$

Use a calculator to solve for *x*.

1. Clear display.   [C]

2. Enter the number 350.   [3] [5] [0]

3. Press the multiplication key.   [×]

4. Enter the number 65.   [6] [5]

5. Press the division key.   [÷]

6. Enter the number 200.   [2] [0] [0]

7. Press the equals key.   [=]

8. Read the answer on the display.   113.75

Moab can expect an increase in yield of about 114 bushels per acre.

EXAMPLE C: Mario wants to measure the height of his house. He knows that the house casts a shadow 85 ft long at 5 o'clock in the afternoon. At the same time, he knows that his 18-foot-tall flagpole casts a shadow 35 ft long. Use this information to calculate the height of Mario's house.

SOLUTION: First, make a diagram of the information you have. For example, Figure 6.2 shows the shadows cast by the house and by the flagpole. It is reasonable to assume a relationship between the height of any structure (a house or a flagpole, for instance) and the length of its shadow.

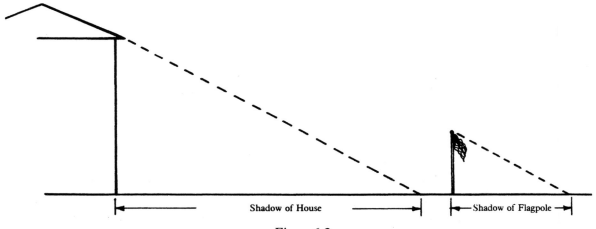

Shadow of House   Shadow of Flagpole

Figure 6.2

Thus, it is possible to say that:

$$\frac{\text{height of house}}{\text{length of house shadow}} = \frac{\text{height of flagpole}}{\text{length of flagpole shadow}}$$

The height of the house *x* is the unknown. Write the proportion:

$$\frac{x}{85'} = \frac{18'}{35'}$$

Cross-multiply:

$$(35') \times (x) = (18') \times (85')$$

Solve for the unknown:

$$x = \frac{(18') \times (85')}{35'}$$

$$x = 43.7'$$

The house is 43.7 ft tall.

Practice Problems

1. Express the ratio of the length of line *a* to the length of line *b* in each of the figures below. Use a ruler to find the length of each line. Change fractions to a decimal equivalent.

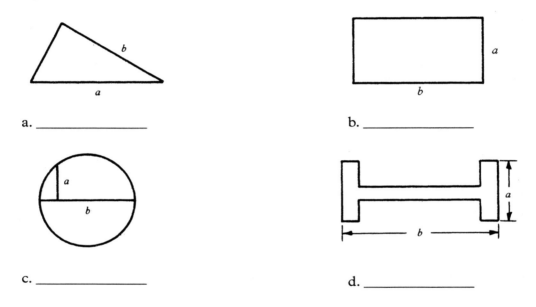

a. _____   b. _____

c. _____   d. _____

2. The data below show the volume of gasoline (gallons) used for various distances (miles) driven by various model cars. Write a ratio for miles driven to gasoline used for each model car. Reduce the ratio to show how many miles are driven for 1 gallon of gasoline.

Model	A	B	C	D	E
Miles Driven	594	564	832.3	720	409.76
Gasoline Used (gal)	18	23.5	29	45	20.8

_____ _____ _____ _____ _____

3. A machine contains five sets of bevel gears. The table below shows the number of teeth in each set of gears. Find the gear ratio in each of these sets. Convert all ratios to the form $a : 1$.

Gear Set	A	B	C	D	E
Gear 1 (number of teeth)	28	32	32	28	25
Gear 2 (number of teeth)	56	96	112	133	110

_____ _____ _____ _____ _____

4. Find the ratios of all possible pairs of resistors shown in the circuit in Figure 6.3. Reduce all ratios to the form $a : 1$.

_____

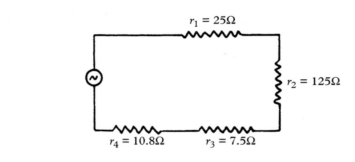

Figure 6.3

5. Mei Li analyzes four samples of brass. Express the composition of each sample as a ratio of copper to zinc. Reduce each fraction to lowest terms.

Sample	A	B	C	D
Copper (g)	18.0	3.240	2.838	5.292
Zinc (g)	6.0	1.215	0.774	2.940

_____ _____ _____ _____

6. The chart below describes five of the transformers on which Naomi works. Calculate the ratio of primary to secondary for each transformer. Express each ratio as a fraction in lowest terms and in the $a : 1$ format.

Transformer Number	3001	3008	3017	3029	3085
Primary (turns)	250	375	340	425	585
Secondary (turns)	120	115	85	$32\frac{1}{2}$	$46\frac{1}{2}$

_____ _____ _____ _____ _____

7. Goran has been asked to calculate in full reams how much paper the office will need in the next 7 months. He knows that 145 reams were used in the first 2 months of the year. How much paper will the office need?

   _____

8. The last time Maurice worked on a housing development, he found that he used 125 pounds of nails on the 3 homes he helped to build. How many pounds of nails should he expect to order for his next job, the construction of 16 houses of the same size and design?

   _____

9. The recipe for the sauce that Elmina usually makes in her catering business is designed for 12 people. Calculate the revised amount of each item from the recipe listed below that she will need for a party of 135 people.

Catsup	100 cc	_____
Tabasco sauce	15 cc	_____
Clam juice	125 cc	_____
Worcestershire sauce	7 cc	_____
Lemon juice	20 cc	_____

10. Nedra has installed four electrical circuits in an office. What is the total resistance of each of the circuits below if 10 linear feet of the wire has a resistance of 1.305 ohms? (1 meter = 3.281 feet)

    Circuit 1: 52.38 m _____

    Circuit 2: 61.94 m _____

    Circuit 3: 46.64 m _____

    Circuit 4: 80.79 m _____

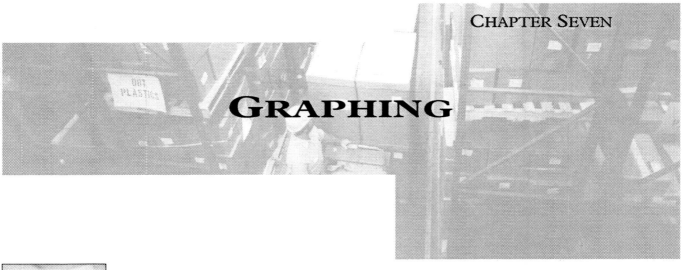

CHAPTER SEVEN

GRAPHING

Learning the Concept

You can represent data in a variety of ways. The weather station where Pauline works, for example, records the temperature every hour all day long. Pauline reads the thermometer at the station, then she writes the temperature in a logbook, as shown below.

6 A.M.	60°	10 A.M.	65°	2 P.M.	70°
7 A.M.	59°	11 A.M.	68°	3 P.M.	67°
8 A.M.	61°	12 noon	71°	4 P.M.	66°
9 A.M.	63°	1 P.M.	71°	5 P.M.	62°

The log book is one way to represent these data. However, Pauline usually puts the data into another format, similar to the table shown below.

Temperatures   May 28

Time	0600	0700	0800	0900	1000	1100	1200	1300	1400	1500	1600	1700
Temp °F	60	59	61	63	65	68	71	71	70	67	66	52

Pauline might also use yet another method to represent the data. She might use a graph. A **graph** is a pictorial method of describing data.

— Types of Graphs —

The kind of graph you choose to make depends on the kind of information you want to illustrate. Among the most common kinds of graphs are circle graphs, bar graphs, and line graphs.

Circle Graphs

Sometimes you need to show a quantity divided into two or more parts. A circle graph illustrates this kind of information. The wedges into which the circle graph is divided show how the total quantity is divided into separate parts.

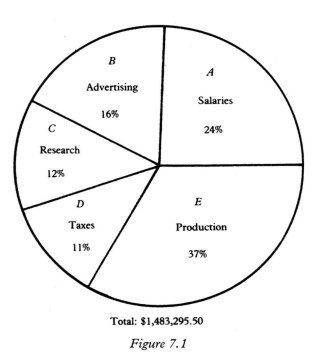

The circle graph shown in Figure 7.1 illustrates how a publishing company spends its money in one year. The whole circle stands for the total amount of money spent by the publisher. The wedge marked *A* shows how much of the company's expenses go to salaries (24%). The wedge marked *B* indicates the amount spent on advertising (16%). Wedges *C*, *D*, and *E* illustrate the fractions of expenses that go toward research, taxes, and production, respectively.

Total: $1,483,295.50

Figure 7.1

If you know the company's total expenses, you can calculate the amount spent on each item from the information in the circle graph.

Salaries (*A*):   24% × $1,483.295.50 = $355,900.92

Advertising (*B*): 16% × $1,483.295.50 = $237,327.28

Research (*C*):   12% × $1,483.295.50 = $177,995.46

Taxes (*D*):   11% × $1,483.295.50 = $163,162.50

Production (*E*):   37% × $1,483.295.50 = $548,819.33

Notice that the circle graph always shows a whole divided into its smaller parts.

Bar Graphs

To understand when to use bar graphs and line graphs, you need to know about data. Data can be classified into two general types: **discrete** (or *discontinuous*) and **continuous.** The publishing company's circle graph contains discrete data. The graph shows that the publishing company spends its money on certain specific categories, such as salaries, advertising, production, taxes, and research. These categories are called discrete or discontinuous because they are totally separate and distinct from one another. Below are other examples of discrete categories:

Colors: red, orange, yellow, blue, green

Months: January, March, May, July, September

Sizes of taper pins: 7/0, 6/0, 5/0, 4/0, 3/0, 2/0

You can count the number of items in any of these discrete categories. For example, you can count the number of 7/0 taper pins used on a job, the number of 6/0 pins, the number of 5/0 pins, and so on.

A bar graph, such as the one shown in Figure 7.2, is the best way to graph discrete data.

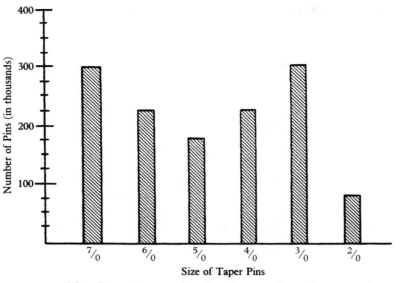

Number of taper pins, by size, produced last month

Figure 7.2

This graph shows the number of taper pins of various sizes sold last month. In this bar graph, the height of each bar stands for the number of items in each category. Note that the graph's framework is made with two lines drawn at right angles to each other. These lines are the **axes** (singular: **axis**) of the graph. When you set out to make a bar graph, your first step is to set up the framework—the axes—for your graph.

The horizontal axis is marked off with one division for each size category of taper pin. The divisions are marked 7/0, 6/0, 5/0, and so on. The vertical axis is marked off to show the quantities of each item. You can see that the divisions are marked with the numbers 100, 200, 300, and so on. Notice the comment in parentheses on the side of the axis: *in thousands*. The comment means that each number on the vertical axis must be multiplied by 1,000. The comment *in thousands* tells you that the first division, marked 100, actually stands for $100 \times 1,000$—or 100,000. The second division, marked 200, actually stands for $200 \times 1,000$—or 200,000. And so on.

Notice that not every division on the vertical axis is labeled. Only certain division lines are marked (100, 200, 300, for example) to keep the graph simple and easy to read. Writing in the value of every division line would make the graph crowded and difficult to read.

Even without labels for every division line, you can figure out what each line stands for. The first labeled division stands for 100,000 taper pins. Between the 0 point on the axis and the 100,000 line there are 4 divisions. Each of these divisions stands for $100,000 \div 4 = 25,000$ taper pins. The first division on the vertical axis represents 25,000 taper pins; the second division stands for 50,000 pins; the third division stands for 75,000 taper pins; and so on.

Line Graphs

The term **continuous data** refers to data in a regular, uninterrupted flow. Pauline's temperature readings at the beginning of this chapter are an example of continuous data. Pauline measured the temperature only once every hour. That doesn't mean that no temperature existed at 7:30 A.M., 8:30 A.M., and so on, . . . or at 7:15 A.M., 7:30 A.M., 7:45 A.M., and so on, . . . or at 7:01 A.M., 7:02 A.M., 7:03 A.M., . . . and so on.

In fact, at any instant, Pauline could have looked at the thermometer and recorded a temperature reading. Some thermometers do just that. Some thermometers automatically record the temperature every second—every fraction of a second—throughout the day. Some other examples of continuous data are water flow through a pipe, electrical current over a circuit, and the noise of a running motor.

A line graph is the best way to represent continuous data. Refer to the line graph (below) of Pauline's data (Figure 7.3) for the discussion that follows.

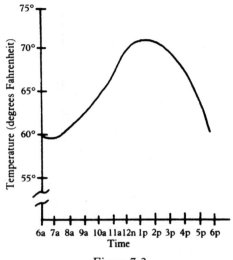

Figure 7.3

Set up a line graph the same way you make a bar graph. Draw two axes and label them with the quantities you are measuring. In Pauline's line graph, the quantities are time and temperature. The horizontal axis is called the *x*-axis, and the vertical axis is called the *y*-axis. Where the axes meet is called the origin (o).

Mark the *x*-axis (time) in divisions that represent hours. Mark the *y*-axis (temperature) in degrees Fahrenheit. Pauline's graph starts with 6 A.M. at the origin and extends to 6 P.M. at the far right of the *x*-axis. Each division represents one hour. Pauline's *y*-axis is marked every 5°F.

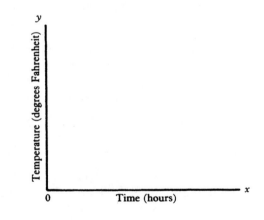

Figure 7.4

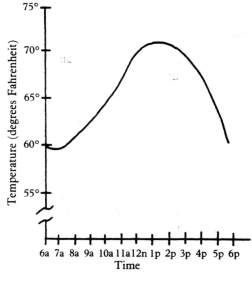

Figure 7.5

Mark off your x- and y-axes. Select units that illustrate your data. There is only one rule: Your divisions must be in the same units all along the axis. Your divisions must be uniform. Dividing the axis as shown in Figure 7.6, for example, is not allowed.

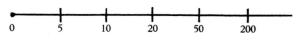

Figure 7.6

Notice the wiggly lines near the bottom of the y-axis in Pauline's graph. The wiggly lines indicate that part of the y-axis—the part from the origin to nearly 55°F—has been cut out. The wiggly lines tell us that there are no data for temperatures less than 59°F. Including lower temperatures on the y-axis would be a waste of space.

You can see how helpful this method can be by making a new graph of Pauline's data using a full y-axis, with all temperature values from 0°F (the origin) to 75°F. Make that graph after you've finished reading the section called "Making a Line Graph." Compare your graph to the one in Figure 7.3. Decide which graph provides a more useful picture of Pauline's data.

— Making a Line Graph —

Draw and label the axes for your line graph, and mark the divisions on each axis. Now you are ready to put data on your graph.

Suppose you want to test the stretch modulus of some copper wire. **Stretch modulus** is a measure of how much a wire lengthens as it is subjected to force. You place weights on the wire and measure its length each time you add weight. The kind of data you might record is shown in the table below. The letter W in the first row stands for the weight (in kilograms) added to the wire. The letter s represents how much (in centimeters) the wire stretches as weight is added.

W (in kg)	200	400	600	800	1,000	1,200	1,400	1,600	1,800	2,000
s (in cm)	1.0	2.0	3.0	4.0	5.0	6.0	7.0	8.0	9.0	10.0

Of the two quantities represented in this table—weight and length—one quantity is completely under your control. That quantity is how much weight you decide to add to the wire. You choose how much weight to put on the wire. The quantity the experimenter controls is called the **independent variable.** In this example, weight W is the independent variable. The independent variable usually appears on the x-axis.

The other quantity is not under the experimenter's control. When you add weight to the wire, you don't choose how much the wire stretches. The weight determines how much the wire stretches. How much the wire stretches depends on how much weight is added. In this example, the stretch s depends on how much weight is added. That is why it's called the **dependent variable.** The dependent variable usually appears on the y-axis.

You can use this information to set up a graph of the data shown in the table above.

Plotting Points

The next step is to convert your data to positions on the graph. Use the table to look at one pair of data at a time. Look at the first pair of data:

$$W = 200 \text{ kg} \qquad s = 1.0 \text{ cm}$$

Think of each pair of data as a single point on the graph. For example, the $W = 200$ kg line intersects (crosses) the $s = 1.0$ cm line at a single point on the graph below (Figure 7.7). Converting data to points on a graph is called **plotting points.**

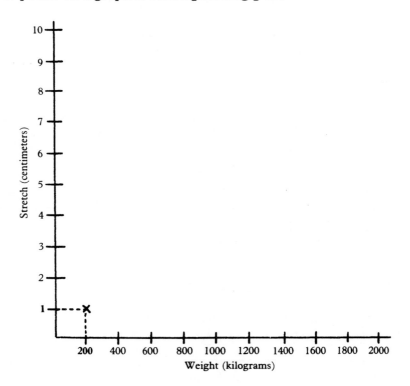

Figure 7.7

Plot the next set of data in the table: Find the point where line $W = 400$ kg intersects line $s = 2.0$ cm (Figure 7.8).

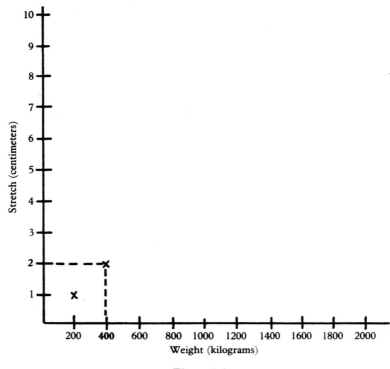

Figure 7.8

Continue to plot one point for each pair of data in the table. The table contains 10 pairs of data. So you will plot 10 points on the graph, as shown in Figure 7.9.

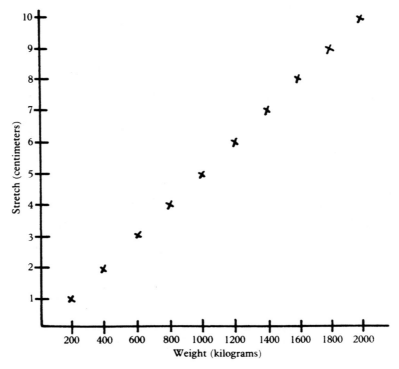

Figure 7.9

Joining the Points

Look at the table. Between 200 kg and 2,000 kg, you measure stretch every time you add another 200 kg. Of course, you know that whatever size weight you decide to add, no matter how large or small, there will be measurable stretch. When you join the points you have plotted, as shown in Figure 7.10, you simply reflect the fact that there is measurable stretch between your data points. You reflect the fact that the data in our example are continuous data.

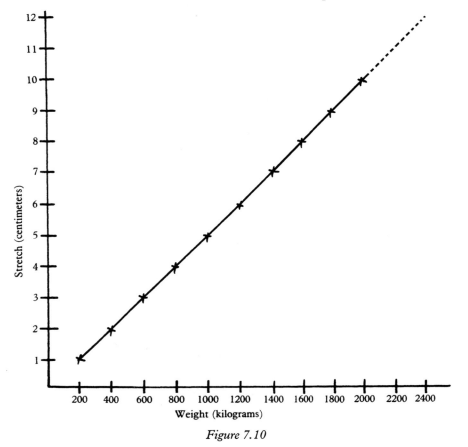

Figure 7.10

The line you have drawn is really a set of many separate points. Each point on the line represents a set of data you *might* have collected. Using your data, the line on the graph is the best picture you can draw of the relationship between weight (*W*) and stretch (*s*).

Best-Fitting Line

Notice that the table of weight and stretch data looks perfect. Notice that for every increase of 200 kg in weight, there is exactly a 1.0-cm increase in stretch. Perfect data make for a nice example, but experiments seldom work out so neatly. Weights are never perfectly accurate. Conditions vary. Humans make mistakes. A more accurate set of data might look more like this.

W (in kg)	200	400	600	800	1,000	1,200	1,400	1,600	1,800	2,000
s (in cm)	1.0	2.1	2.9	4.2	5.0	5.8	7.2	8.1	9.1	10.2

To plot this data, put one point on the graph for each set of data in the table. In this case, you can see that the points on the graph are not in a straight line (Figure 7.11).

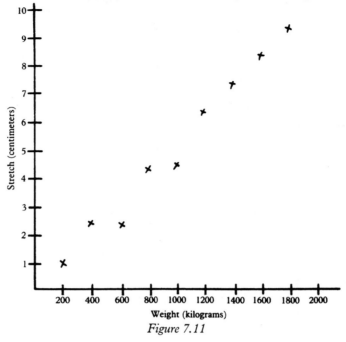

Figure 7.11

How will you connect these points?

One possibility is simply to join the data points, as you would in a connect-the-dots puzzle. Taken together, the points *almost* form a straight line.

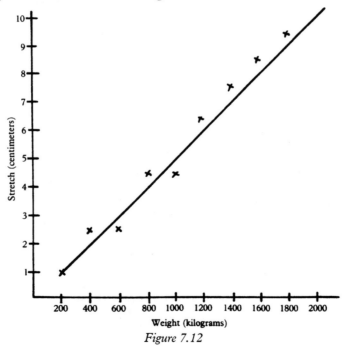

Figure 7.12

In a "perfect" experiment, the data points would form a straight line. In real life, you must find a line that comes close to your data points. You find the **best-fitting line** (Figure 7.12). The best-fitting line for our graph is the one we drew with the perfect data (where for every 200-kg increase in weight, there was exactly a 1.0-cm increase in stretch). In the real world, you don't know the perfect answer in advance. You have to make some guesses to decide what the best-fitting line will look like. The better your original data, the easier it is to determine the best-fitting line.

Using a Line Graph

You may be asked to make graphs or to read and interpret them. For example, Figure 7.13 shows temperature change on a wing section as a jet's speed increases.

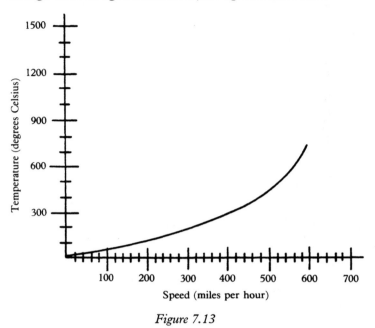

Figure 7.13

Use this graph to determine the temperature of the wing section when the plane is traveling at 400 miles per hour (mph).

Find the point marked 400 mph on the *x*-axis (Figure 7.14). Read up to the curved line on the graph.

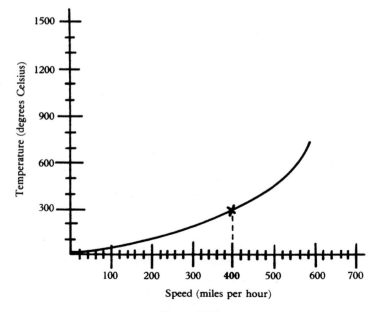

Figure 7.14

Follow the dotted line from this point on the curve to where the dotted line intersects the *y*-axis (Figure 7.15). That point (300°C) is the wing temperature as the plane reaches 400 mph.

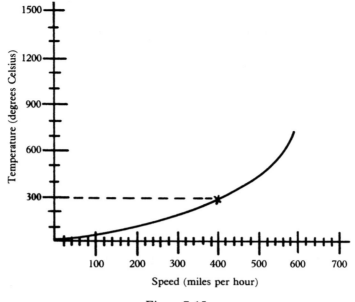

Figure 7.15

The point on the graph where 400 mph and 300°C meet represents a set of data like any other data, such as Pauline's temperature records or the stress-modulus data.

You can use the same graph to answer the question: At what speed is the wing section's temperature 535°C? Estimate the location of 535°C on the *y*-axis. From that point, read across to the curve, and from there read straight down to the *x*-axis. You will find a speed of about 440 mph. You can use the graph below to answer the question: At 440 mph, the temperature of the plane's wing section rises to 535°C (Figure 7.16).

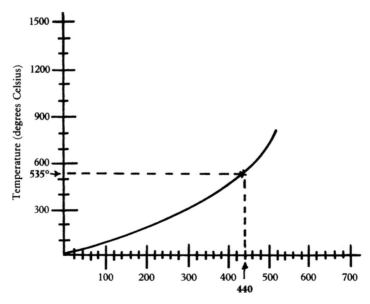

Figure 7.16

Extrapolating from a Line Graph

Graphs are sometimes used to make predictions. Look at the graph in Figure 7.17.

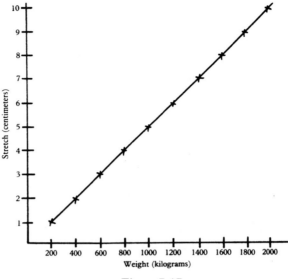

Figure 7.17

That graph shows the stretch in copper wire as weights up to 2,000 kg are added to it. You might want to use the graph to predict how much the wire would stretch if you add more than 2,000 kg.

The dotted line in Figure 7.18 predicts what will happen *if* the wire continues to behave under greater weight as it does with weights of less than 2,000 kg.

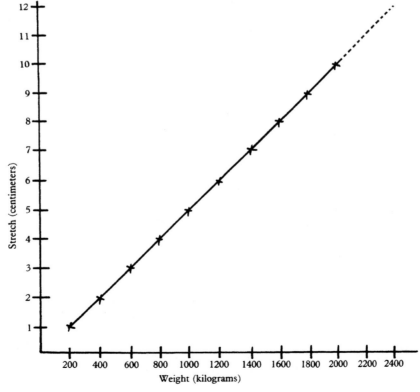

Figure 7.18

If that assumption is true, then a load of 2,400 kg should cause the wire to stretch to 12 cm.

Making a guess about conditions beyond—but based on—those that have been measured is called **extrapolation.** Extrapolation is always a guess—and even a guess based on good information is still a guess. Extrapolation is a guess based on the assumption that conditions expressed by the graph do not change.

At some point, that assumption will fail. You cannot keep adding weights to the copper wire forever. At some point the wire will break. You may extrapolate a stretch of 15 cm at 3,000 kg. But if the wire actually breaks at 2,800 kg, your guess doesn't mean much. Guessing by extrapolation has only a limited usefulness.

Curved-line graphs like the graph in Figure 7.19 present another issue.

Beyond 700 mph, close to the speed of sound, for example, metal begins to act in ways that are harder to predict. Figure 7.19 shows that this uncertainty limits the usefulness of extrapolating the curve beyond 700 mph. Beyond 700 mph, conditions change, so there is more than one possibility.

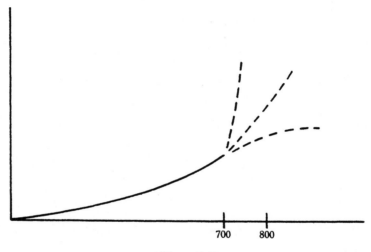

Figure 7.19

— Solved Examples —

EXAMPLE A: Use the data below to construct a circle graph of the age distribution of workers in the Hayes-Shelling company.

Age Group	18–27	28–37	38–47	48–57	58+
Number of Workers	32	48	58	46	39

SOLUTION: Begin by changing the number of workers in each age group to a percentage of the whole. (Round off to the nearest whole number.) The total number of workers in the company is: 32 + 48 + 58 + 46 + 39 = 223. So the percentage in each age group is as follows:

$$18\text{–}27: \frac{32}{223} \times 100\% = 14\%$$

$$28\text{–}37: \frac{48}{223} \times 100\% = 22\%$$

$$38\text{–}47: \frac{58}{223} \times 100\% = 26\%$$

$$48-57: \frac{46}{223} \times 100\% = 21\%$$

$$58+: \frac{39}{223} \times 100\% = 17\%$$

Draw the circle graph so that 14% of the circle stands for the 18–27 age group, 22% for the 28–37 age group, and so on.

The key idea is that every circle contains 360°.

By rounding off to the nearest whole, you can represent the 18–27 age group with a wedge that is 14% × 360°, the 28–37 age group with a wedge that is 22% × 360°, and so on, as follows:

$$18-27: 14\% \times 360° = 50°$$

$$28-37: 22\% \times 360° = 79°$$

$$38-47: 26\% \times 360° = 94°$$

$$48-57: 21\% \times 360° = 76°$$

$$58+: 17\% \times 360° = 61°$$

Draw the circle that will become your graph. Then draw any radius of your circle, as shown in Figure 7.20.

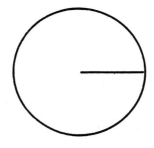

Figure 7.20

A **central angle** is an angle whose vertex is at the center of a circle. With a protractor, lay out a central angle equal to 50° (Figure 7.21). This 50° wedge represents the 18–27 age group (14%) because 50° is 14% of 360°.

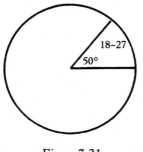

Figure 7.21

Use your protractor on either radius to lay out another central angle, this one equal to 79° (Figure 7.22). This second wedge represents the 28–37 age group.

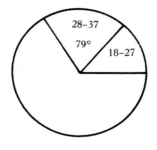

Figure 7.22

Repeat the process. Construct central angles equal to 94°, 76°, and 61° to represent the 38–47, 48–57, and 58+ age groups. Your finished graph will look like Figure 7.23.

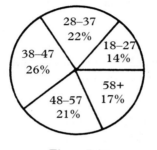

Figure 7.23

EXAMPLE B: Determine the Bossey Company's profit (in dollars) from each source in the circle graph (Figure 7.24). Total profit last year was $164,238.94.

Figure 7.24

SOLUTION: The circle graph shows the percent profit from each source. To find the dollar amount, multiply each percent times the total profit. (Round your answers to the nearest cent.)

Retail sales:	24.8% × $164,238.94 = $40,731.26
Wholesale sales:	65.3% × $164,238.94 = $107,248.02
Investments:	9.9% × $164,238.94 = $16,259.66

EXAMPLE C: Use the information in the table below to make a bar graph that shows how many telephone calls Yoshi has answered in the last three months.

Week	Number of Calls	Week	Number of Calls	Week	Number of Calls
3/8	32	4/5	18	5/3	64
3/15	37	4/12	40	5/10	21
3/22	68	4/19	35	5/17	28
3/29	35	4/26	42	5/24	34

SOLUTION: Draw and label the axes for your graph on grid paper. Label the *x*-axis for the week and the *y*-axis for the phone calls.

Use the grid paper's horizontal and vertical lines to mark off your axes. Divide the *x*-axis into 12 equal sections, one for each week. Then select a scale that allows you to fit all the phone calls on the *y*-axis and still have bars large enough to read easily.

Look at the table. The largest number of phone calls is 68. So you might choose 70 as the highest number on your *y*-axis. You might divide the *y*-axis into 7 equal sections, as shown in Figure 7.25. If space permits, you might mark each of these sections in smaller units.

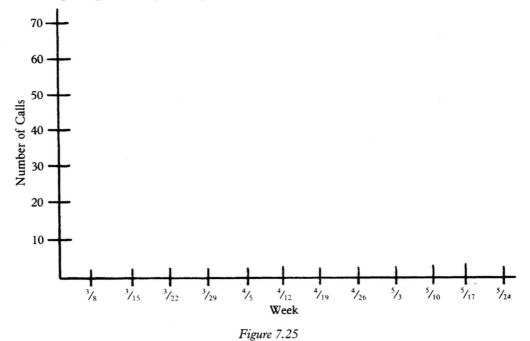

Figure 7.25

If you use grid paper like the example in Figure 7.26, with about 30 squares on one side and about 40 squares on the other side, you can divide the *x*-axis into sections 2 squares wide. The 40 squares on the *y*-axis will allow plenty of room to represent the phone calls. Start at the origin, and mark off 5 squares for each of your 7 sections (5 squares × 7 sections = 35 squares). Label each section (10, 20, etc.) as in Figure 7.26. A single square stands for one-fifth the distance between your number-labeled lines, or $\frac{1}{5} \times 10 = 2$. Each square on the *y*-axis, then, stands for 2 phone calls.

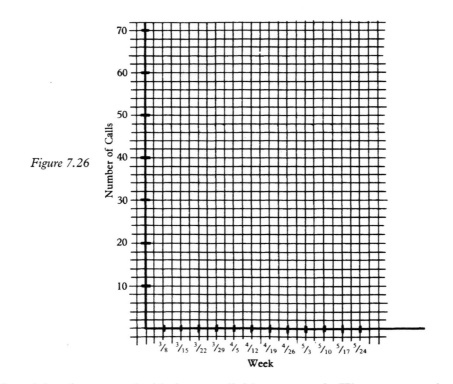

Figure 7.26

Use trial and error to decide how to divide up an axis. The more graphs you make, the better you get at making these decisions.

Now you are ready to put in the bars. Look at the information for the first date in the table. During the week of March 8, Yoshi answered 32 calls. Find the line representing 32 on the y-axis. The line representing 30 is marked. Remember that each square on the y-axis stands for two calls, so the mark on the graph corresponds to 32 telephone calls (Figure 7.27).

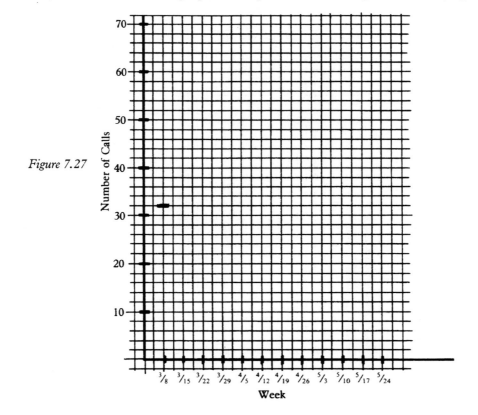

Figure 7.27

Notice that this mark is directly above the corresponding date, 3/8, on the *x*-axis. This mark will be the top of the first bar, as shown in Figure 7.28. Use the grid to draw a bar wide enough to be seen easily without running over into the next space.

Figure 7.28

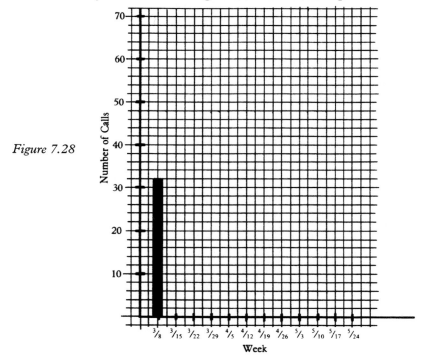

Go on to the next date. The number of calls during the week of 3/15 was 37. The position that corresponds to 37 on the *y*-axis is the mark at 30 plus 3 more squares (3 × 2 calls per square = 6 calls) plus $\frac{1}{2}$ of another square ($\frac{1}{2}$ × 2 calls per square = 1 call): 30 + 6 + 1 = 37 calls. Mark this position on the *y*-axis. Then draw a bar vertically from the 3/15 date on the *x*-axis to your mark. Figure 7.29 shows the first two bars in your graph.

Figure 7.29

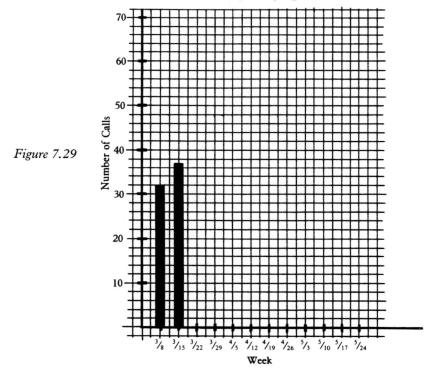

Continue this process with each set of data until you have a complete bar graph like the one shown in Figure 7.30.

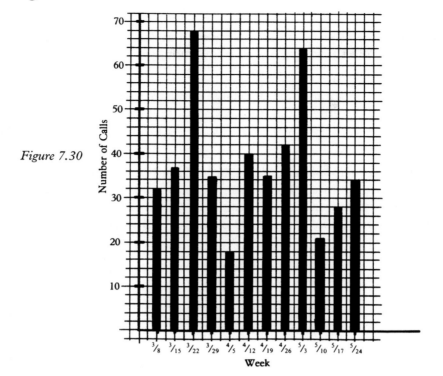

Figure 7.30

EXAMPLE D: Amanda uses the bar graph in Figure 7.31 to determine how many brochures to mail out to each city shown on the graph. She divides the population of each city by 250 to determine how many brochures to send out. How many brochures will she need for each of the following cities: Grand Forks, Grand Rapids, and Grand Island?

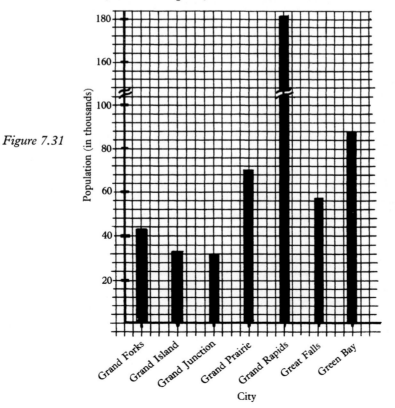

Figure 7.31

SOLUTION: Take a moment to look at the graph. The names of the cities, each with its own bar, appear along the x-axis. The population is given, in thousands, along the y-axis. That means that 20 on the y-axis stands for 20,000, and 40 stands for 40,000, and so on.

Notice that the distance between each marked population line (20 to 40, 40 to 60, 60 to 80, etc.) contains 5 squares. So 5 squares = 20,000 population, and 1 square = 20,000 ÷ 5 = 4,000 population.

Notice that the population of Grand Rapids is large compared with the others. To fit Grand Rapids on the same scale with the other cities, the y-axis would have to be very long. But if we break the y-axis at 100,000, as indicated by the wavy lines, the Grand Rapids population fits without losing any information.

The populations of three cities appear on the graph: Grand Forks, Grand Island, and Grand Rapids. Look at the bar for Grand Forks. What is the population represented by the Grand Forks bar? To answer that question, lay a straight edge across the top of the bar, and see where it intersects the y-axis. You'll find that the top of the bar falls just below the 44,000 mark on the y-axis. A reasonable estimate might be 43,500.

By a similar process, you should be able to estimate the population of Grand Island at about 33,000 and that of Grand Rapids at about 181,000.

Finally, the problem tells you that Amanda divides the population of each city by 250. So the number of brochures needed for each city is as follows:

Grand Forks: 43,500 ÷ 250 = 174 brochures

Grand Island: 33,000 ÷ 250 = 132 brochures

Grand Rapids: 181,000 ÷ 250 = 724 brochures

EXAMPLE E: Grant has measured the number of fruit flies surviving in a container after various doses of pesticide. The table below summarizes his results. Make a line graph that illustrates his data.

Dose (in mg)	0	1.0	1.5	2.5	5.0	10.0	20.0
Number of Flies Surviving	300	210	188	150	98	34	9

SOLUTION: On grid paper, draw and label the x- and y-axes. Put the dose (mg) (the *independent* variable) on the x-axis. Put the number of surviving fruit flies (the *dependent* variable) on the y-axis.

Select an appropriate scale for each axis. Use the 40 squares on your x-axis to represent the dose data (from 0 mg to 20 mg). Each square can stand for 20 mg ÷ 40 spaces = 0.5 mg per space. Use the 30 squares on your y-axis to represent the number of surviving fruit flies (from 9 to 300). Each square can stand for 300 flies ÷ 30 squares = 10 flies per square.

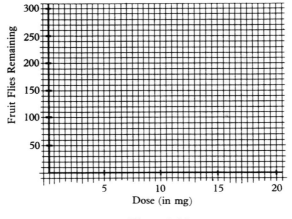

Figure 7.32

Now you can plot one point for each pair of data in the table. Notice that the first point corresponds to a dose of 0 mg and a population of 300 fruit flies. The second point corresponds to a dose of 1.0 mg and a population of 210 fruit flies. The third point corresponds to a dose of 1.5 mg and a population of 188 fruit flies. If you continue plotting points, you get the graph in Figure 7.33.

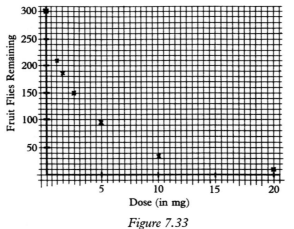

Figure 7.33

Your final step is to find the curve that best fits these points. The graph in Figure 7.34 shows that curve. Notice that the curve does not pass through every point, but comes close to all of them. The curve shows the relationship between pesticide dose and survival of fruit flies.

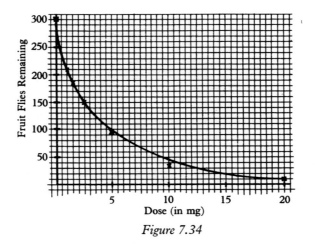

Figure 7.34

EXAMPLE F: The driving efficiency of a certain model automobile, measured in miles per gallon of gasoline at various speeds, is graphed in Figure 7.35. Answer the following questions about this graph.

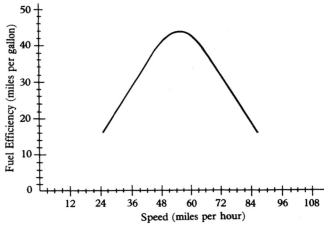

Figure 7.35

1. What is the maximum fuel efficiency? At what speed is this efficiency obtained?

2. What is the minimum fuel efficiency? At what speed is this efficiency obtained?

3. For a person who drives at a constant speed of 65 mph (miles per hour), what fuel efficiency should be expected?

4. If the speed/fuel efficiency pattern shown here is also true below 25 mph and above 85 mph, what fuel efficiency is to be expected at 15 mph?

SOLUTION: Look at the graph. The *y*-axis (fuel efficiency) is laid off in units of miles per gallon (mpg). The first division, marked 10, is the fifth line. So you can see that 5 lines = 10 mpg, or 1 line = 10 mpg ÷ 5 lines = 2 mpg per line. The *x*-axis (speed) is labeled in miles per hour (mph). The first division, labeled 12, is the fourth line. So you can see that 4 lines = 12 mph, or 1 line = 12 mph ÷ 4 lines = 3 mph.

Question 1. The maximum fuel efficiency is the highest point on the graph. Lay a straight edge parallel to the *x*-axis so that it just touches the highest point on the graph. You can read the fuel efficiency at the point where the straight edge intersects the *y*-axis. The point is the second line above 40:

$$40 + (2 \times 2) \text{ mpg} = 44 \text{ mpg}$$

To find the corresponding speed, just rotate the straight edge so that it lies parallel to the *y*-axis at the maximum point on the graph. Then read the speed that corresponds to this point on the *x*-axis. That speed is about 55 mph.

Question 2. The minimum fuel efficiency is represented by the lowest point on the graph. In this case, there appear to be two lowest points, one at each end of the graph. Lay a straight edge on the graph at the low points, first parallel to the *x*-axis, then parallel to the *y*-axis. The minimum fuel efficiency appears to be 16 mpg. The speeds at which this efficiency is achieved are about 24 mph (left) and 87 mph (right).

Question 3. To find the fuel efficiency that corresponds to a driving speed of 65 mph, lay a straight edge on the graph parallel to the *y*-axis. Move the straight edge so that it lies exactly on the 65-mph point.

To estimate this point, between 63 mph and 66 mph, make an *X* on the graph at the point where the straight edge crosses the *x*-axis. Then rotate the straight edge so that it lies parallel to the *x*-axis. The point at which the straight edge intersects the *y*-axis is about 38 mpg.

Question 4. Extrapolate the known data to speeds above and below what was actually measured. Assume that the curve continues in an unchanged pattern at both ends. Lay a straight edge along the curve and draw a dotted line to extend the curve in both directions (Figure 7.36).

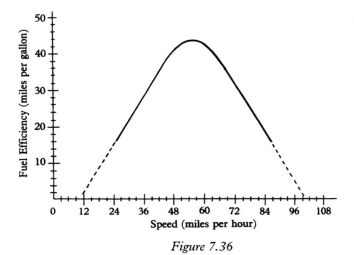

Figure 7.36

To find the fuel efficiency at 15 mph, use the same procedure as above. Lay a straight edge parallel to the *y*-axis. Make an *X* on the dotted line part of the curve, rotate the straight edge, and read the corresponding fuel efficiency on the *y*-axis (about 6 mpg).

Practice Problems

1. Make a circle graph to represent the data as a percentage of the whole in each of the examples below. Round your answers to the nearest whole number. Label each wedge in your graph.

   a. Rozelia's family grows 430 acres of alfalfa, 180 acres of corn, and 320 acres of wheat.

   b. Last year, the Jennings and Fong Chemical Company produced 4,875 pounds of inorganic chemicals, 8,295 pounds of organic chemicals, 925 pounds of agricultural chemicals, and 1,265 pounds of plastic.

   c. Last year, expenses for Lorna's electrical-repair business fell into the categories of materials ($35,882), salaries ($69,483), taxes ($9,778), supplies ($4,836), and advertising ($2,617).

   d. Demetrio's trucking firm operates four trucks. Last year each truck made several trips. The number of trips each truck made are arranged by distance in the table below. Draw a circle graph to show the *combined* number of trips at *each distance* (for example, 0–50 miles, 51–100 miles) as fraction (percent) of the total distance logged by all four trucks for the whole year.

Truck	0–50 mi	51–100 mi	101–200 mi	201–500 mi	Over 500 mi
1	3	8	17	21	5
2	12	4	15	30	6
3	8	12	25	21	7
4	7	21	30	11	3

   e. Sathya must assign space in the building he is designing: 480 sq ft for offices, 3,050 sq ft for commercial display, 1,795 sq ft for storage, 565 sq ft for hallways and passages, and 325 sq ft for personal areas. (Round your answers to the nearest whole number.)

2. The circle graph in Figure 7.37 shows the number of people making each salary at the Piang Construction Company. How many employees are there in each of the categories shown? (Round your answers to the nearest whole number.)

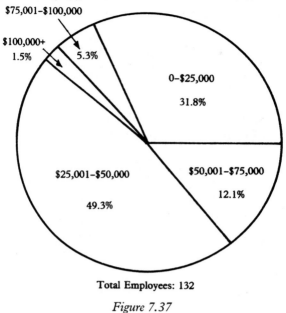

Total Employees: 132

Figure 7.37

3. The circle graph in Figure 7.38 shows the bolts ordered from Isamu's company last year. How many of the best-selling and how many of the poorest-selling sizes were ordered? (Round your answers to the nearest whole number.)

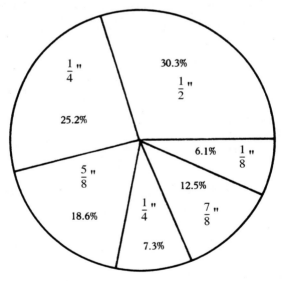

Total Sales: 68,495 Bolts

Figure 7.38

4. Construct a bar graph that illustrates each of the examples below. Label your axes and each of the bars.

   a. The catering service run by Joan and Justo served the following number of meals during each of the last six months:

Month	March	April	May	June	July	August
Number of Meals	240	318	425	306	125	138

   b. Grace is in charge of a computer-console production team that has turned out a record number of units in all but two of the weeks shown in the table below.

Week	9/8	9/15	9/22	9/29	10/6	10/13	10/20
Number of Units	205	215	220	175	160	245	255

   c. Jorge is in charge of ordering insulation at the shop. The data below summarize his orders for recent months.

May:	4,850 rolls	September:	10,125 rolls
June:	5,975 rolls	October:	8,425 rolls
July:	9,160 rolls	November:	2,160 rolls
August:	9,425 rolls	December:	975 rolls

   d. Gustave works as a carpenter in a housing development. He measures oak, pine, and walnut to build each of the four designs listed in the table below. Make a bar graph that shows (in board feet) how much of each type of wood Gustave uses.

Type of Wood	The Atlantic	The Belvedere	The Clarion	The Dynasty
oak	200	400	750	1,875
pine	1,500	1,800	2,125	2,000
walnut	0	100	250	550

   e. The cost per kilogram of the metal Midge has used in her shop over a decade is shown below.

1993: $3.85	1998: $3.71
1994: $3.79	1999: $3.99
1995: $3.71	2000: $3.99
1996: $3.59	2001: $4.58
1997: $3.57	2002: $4.73

5. The melting points, in degrees Celsius, of various alloys are shown in the bar graph in Figure 7.39. Which alloy has the highest melting point? What is the melting point of that alloy? Express the difference in melting point, in degrees Celsius, if you substituted Constantan for stainless steel in a new product.

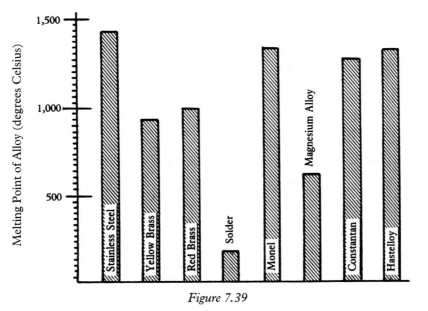

Figure 7.39

6. Simon tries to allot about half as much time to teaching flying as he does to his commercial flying jobs. Use the graph shown in Figure 7.40 to answer the following questions.

   a. How many hours did he spend teaching in May?

   b. How many hours did he spend on commercial jobs in July?

   c. In which month(s) did he spend more time teaching than he had planned?

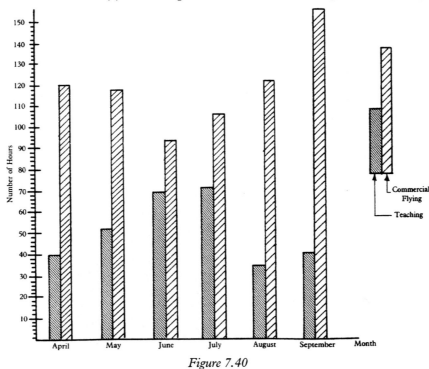

Figure 7.40

7. Construct a line graph to illustrate each of the following examples. Label your axes. Find the best-fitting line to illustrate the data.

a. At Melva's auto shop, workers use the table below to determine the charge on one cell in a battery.

Specific Gravity of Battery Fluid	1.245	1.255	1.265	1.275	1.285	1.295	1.305
Charge on Battery (in volts)	1.35	1.63	1.80	1.91	1.96	1.99	2.01

b. Hattie installs sprinkler systems in her clients' gardens. The table below shows how water flow varies, depending on what size pipe Hattie uses.

Pipe Diameter (cm)	1.0	1.5	2.0	2.5	3.0	3.5	4.0	4.5	5.0
Water flow (L/min)	4.0	9.0	15.0	25.0	35.0	50.0	65.0	80.0	100.0

c. The yield (in pounds/acre) from Stanley's sunflower farm depends on how much fertilizer he uses (in pounds/acre), as shown in the table below.

Fertilizer (pounds/acre)	Yield (pounds/acre)	Fertilizer (pounds/acre)	Yield (pounds/acre)
0	400	200	2,000
25	590	225	1,995
50	805	250	2,005
75	990	275	1,995
100	1,200	300	2,000
125	1,395	325	1,845
150	1,610	350	1,704
175	1,810	375	1,545

8. The graph in Figure 7.41 shows how much time Alessandrio needs to cut through steel, using flames at various temperatures. Answer the following questions about the graph.

   a. How long will it take to cut through the metal using a flame at the highest temperature shown on the graph? At the lowest temperature?

   b. How long will it take if Alessandrio uses a torch at 1,800°C?

   c. How hot must the torch be to cut through the metal in 4 minutes?

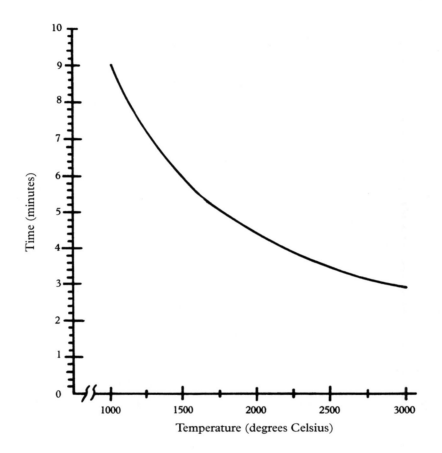

Figure 7.41

9. Vadim works with stage lights. Light intensity varies with distance (of the light source) from center stage, as shown in Figure 7.42. Use the graph to answer the following questions.

    a. How much light is available from a spotlight placed 20 feet from center stage? 40 feet from center stage?

    b. How far from center stage can a light be placed to get a relative intensity of 10%? A relative intensity of 33%?

    c. Predict the relative intensity of a light placed 60 feet from center stage.

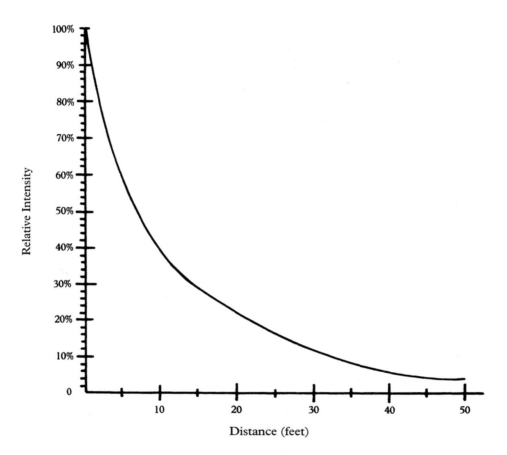

Figure 7.42

10. Figure 7.43 shows how much coal miners at the Four Square Mine produced over a period of years.

   a. How much coal did they produce in each of the following years? 1955, 1970, 1985, and 2000?

   b. In what year did the miners produce 50,000 tons? 75,000 tons? 100,000 tons?

   c. How much coal will the miners produce in 2005? In 2010? In 2015? Show how you might make two different predictions for each of these years.

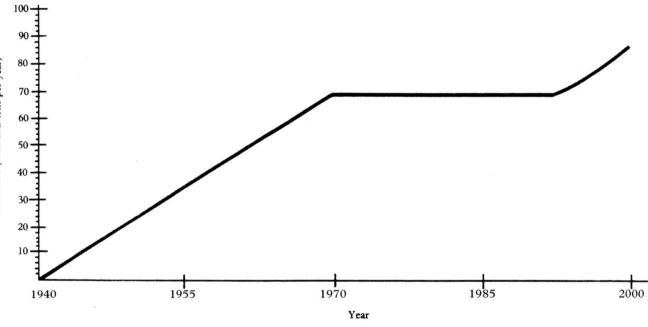

Figure 7.43